The Complete
Church Newsletter

The Complete Church Newsletter

A Guide to Starting, Strengthening, Renovating, or Resurrecting

Jeffery P. Dennis

BAKER BOOK HOUSE
Grand Rapids, Michigan 49516

Contents

Introduction

Does Your Church
Need a Newsletter?

Chances are the list of priorities for your church includes a short entry toward the bottom: "think church newsletter." Often pastors and other church leaders consider newsletters little more than written versions of the Sunday morning announcements, helpful for congregations with thousands of members and dozens of organizations to keep track of, but superfluous for medium-sized and smaller congregations. In fact, the newsletter can play a vital role in the mission of every church, from tiny storefront missions to the ten-thousand-member St. Everybody's-on-the-Green. It can do the following:

> Welcome visitors, make them feel comfortable with the new names and faces they encounter in the church, and encourage them to visit again.
>
> Inform prospective members of the opportunities for Christian growth, service, and fellowship in your church.

Assure shut-ins that they are still an important part of the church family.

Assure former members that they haven't been forgotten by the church community, keep them in touch with their former friends and associates, and encourage them to rejoin the church should their circumstances change.

Reach out to other churches and community organizations as part of an exchange of ideas and information about fellowship, social action, and evangelization.

Inform the unchurched in the community of your church's special outreach and encourage them to visit.

Awaken an interest in spiritual things in the unchurched, gently chide them if they have neglected their spiritual well-being, and encourage them to seek out God's will for their lives.

Inform average church members of opportunities for growth, service, and fellowship that they may have overlooked.

Make average church members feel part of important events happening in the Christian community on the local, national, and international levels.

Inspire and inform children, teenagers, college students, single adults, the elderly, and other groups within the congregation.

Make church members feel that they are making a vital contribution to the growth of the church community, even if they never contribute a word to the newsletter.

Provide a written record of upcoming activities and events for ready reference.

Provide quick and accurate information on the service times and locations, telephone numbers and office hours of the pastoral staff, and crisis contacts.

With a little advance planning, a well-written, professional-looking newsletter is within the reach of any congregation.

The Right Newsletter for the Right Church

1

Many church newsletters fail to elicit much interest, because they contain mainly brief, chatty items about whose son is entering seminary and who was elected president of the Bible League. This may be fine for those few members of the church who have been around since New Testament times and knew the entering seminarian when he was in diapers, but it tends to bore everyone else. Any visitors who wander into the sanctuary and pick up the *First Church Tattler* may suspect that your church is dominated by cliques and in-groups (and they may be right).

There is nothing wrong with devoting space to upcoming church activities and events, but if you want to capture the interest and enthusiasm of the average church member (who hears about upcoming events every Sunday anyway), your newsletter should include denominational, United States, and world religious news and leave room for the thoughts and creative efforts of the congregation. Visitors and prospective members might be more interested in finding out how your church can meet their social, emotional, and spiritual needs. The unchurched might want to see inspirational articles, articles on salvation and the Christian life, and maybe a little humor.

The first rule they teach you in freshman composition class is this: Write for your audience. For example, the simplest Bible study needs to be modified considerably for different audiences. Think of delivering a speech on the Beatitudes consecutively to junior-high Sunday school students, theology professors, or Tibetan monks. Of course, every newsletter fills a variety of needs, but determining your primary audience in advance will help you decide which articles to run in which issue, which article should lead off the front cover, and which should be relegated to the inside back cover under "Notes and Quotes."

Ten Basic Types of Newsletter Pieces

Some of these types are useful for audiences composed primarily of regular church members, while others seem tailor-made for prospective members, visitors, former members, or the unchurched. A few types, borrowed from the newsletters used in business and industry, appear in church newsletters from time to time without benefiting anyone.

Events announcements detail upcoming events and activities that have already received attention in the Sunday bulletin or the announcement section of the Sunday morning service: "Potluck Planned for April 16"; "New Pastor Installation Set for June 4"; "Don't Forget Easter Sunrise Service." Sometimes they advertise ongoing concerns of the congregation rather than events: "Have You Looked at the Building Fund Pledges Lately?"; "Committee to Investigate Color of New Hymnal Covers"; "Church Newsletter Needs (Wants, Desires, Is Desperate For) Writers." These articles can be as important as the Sunday sermon or the after-service fellowship hour in attracting new members, since visitors and prospective members often read them carefully to "get a feel" for how they could become involved in the church community. Even though they hear about every upcoming event two or three times, most regular members of the congregation also find these articles important; they want to have important information about times, dates, and locations written down in a form more permanent than scribbles on the back of a Sunday bulletin.

Unfortunately, events announcements tend to sound superfluous to those who do not attend or plan to attend your church on a regular basis. They may alienate individuals contacted through personal evangelism efforts, who often think of churches as clique-ridden country clubs, and they may depress the shut-ins, who won't be able to attend any of the wonderful upcoming activities.

Individual announcements describe the concerns and activities of individual members of the congregation, rather than the congregation as a whole: "Charles Swanson, son of Arthur and Myra Swanson, Elected to Dean's List at Glory Bible College"; "Ida Phelps Steps down as Missionary Society President, will not Accept Third Term"; "Max Rosenthal Hospitalized for Bunion Surgery." This category also includes monthly recognition of birthdays and anniversaries, honors and awards, students leaving for college this fall, and "Thanks for the Flowers on the Altar to. . . . "

While these articles may be of extreme interest to their subjects, plus relatives and a few close friends, they generate about as much interest as you would expect from the rest of the world. When was the last time you really read the "Thank You for the Flowers" article all the way through? Consequently, individual announcements rarely belong on the most visible pages of the newsletter, the front cover and the back cover. Intersplicing them with events announcements on inner pages is fine. Putting them all together in a block of text on a less visible page, such as the right inner page, is better.

Creative pieces by members of the congregation, chiefly poems, prayers, and very short prose meditations ("The Tomb is Empty"; "Let's Put Christ Back in Christmas"; "Children's Laughter"; "My Thoughts This Mother's Day"), are similar to individual announcements: generally unread except by the authors and their close friends. You can expect them to be of rather poor literary quality. The professionally trained writer in your congregation probably expends his or her creative energies on stories for *The Atlantic Monthly*, not on six-line poems about springtime for the *Bethany Baptist Gazette*.

However, the function of creative pieces in the church newsletter is not to discover new Mark Twains and Edmund Wilsons; it is to make the person who submits a poem feel like an important part of the church community and to inspire others to active participation in both the newsletter and the church. The world's worst poem can do that as well as a Shakespearean sonnet.

Creative pieces submitted by members of the congregation do not often inspire or inform newsletter audiences, so you should probably use no more than one or two per four-page newsletter, or two or three per eight-page newsletter. Do not put any on the front cover, lest visitors get the impression that your newsletter is really a front for the Thursday Afternoon Tea and Iambic Pentameter League. Instead, intersplice them with the other articles in the newsletter, where they can break up long blocks of text to produce a pleasing variety.

Rarely does the church newsletter have room for fiction of any sort. Few writers can pull off an interesting, inspirational short story in 1,000 words or less, and those who can deserve payment for their efforts. Tell them to ship off their submissions to *The Moody Monthly* or *Aglow*, and reserve the pages of the newsletter for other types of articles.

Surveys ("My Favorite Thanksgiving Memory"; "How I Witness at Work"; "My New Year's Resolutions") are actually very brief interviews. Members of the congregation selected at random or restricted to a certain age, marital status, or Sunday school class are asked to respond to a single question, and a few of the resulting answers are published in list form. This type of article generates the same kind of interest as individual announcements or creative pieces, but has a wider appeal, since, presumably, more people are involved. Visitors, prospective members, and the unchurched may be less interested, since they are probably not acquainted with any of the respondents.

Surveys are usually organized as series of short paragraphs, so they can provide the same visual variety as creative pieces and fillers. Intersplice them with the more substantial articles on the inner pages of the newsletter.

News from beyond the confines of the local church is the key to an enthusiastic newsletter readership. It includes events in the national and international religious world, as well as news of other churches in your city or denomination. Since religious stories are about as common as happy endings in secular news media, they generate interest in all audiences. A front cover article about a national or international religious event, particularly one that hasn't appeared on "Eyewitness

News at Ten" yet ("Lutheran Synods Discuss Ordination of Women"; "National Survey Finds Belief in Heaven on the Rise"; "Chaplains Note Evangelistic Revival in the Military") can make your newsletter.

Local religious news articles about churches and religious organizations in your area regardless of denomination ("First Methodist Raises $30,000 in Food Drive"; "Pastor of Calvary Baptist Meets with the Mayor's Committee on Homelessness"; "Renowned Theologian to Speak at Wesley Seminary") are welcome to all audiences. You may want to be careful, though—visitors and prospective members may read the articles and decide to join First Methodist or Calvary Baptist instead.

Denominational news stories often excite longstanding members, as well as those who have transferred from other local churches within your denomination and want to know what your conference or district is up to. Generally, however, their appeal is as limited as that of individual announcements to visitors, prospective members, and the unchurched (unless, of course, they have some background in your denomination).

Most news stories belong on the front cover or interspliced with the events announcements and creative pieces on inner pages of the newsletter.

Personality profiles are short biographies of outstanding (living) religious leaders, and sometimes ordinary Christians, based on personal interviews, which can be augmented by library research. They can grab the attention of all readers if they profile religious leaders beyond the local church: the Methodist bishop who has made a statement against abortion, a professor at a nearby seminary who has written a new book on Ecclesiastes, the born-again star of a popular TV sitcom. Unfortunately, it's quite difficult to get interviews with actors, authors, and other celebrities, and those writers who do land interviews should, again, submit their articles to mass-market periodicals such as *The Moody Magazine*, not the *Fifteenth-Street Pentecostal Tribune*.

Profiles of local church leaders (the pastor, the choir director, a Sunday school teacher), whom regular members see every Sunday and visitors don't know from Malachi, can be tedious. Restrict local profiles to new members of the congregation (if your congregation is *very* small) or new members of the pastoral staff. Alternately, run profiles of several local church leaders in a roundup issue: "Getting to Know Your Pastoral Staff"; "Your Church Organizations and Their Organizers"; "And You Thought You Knew Your Sunday School."

Inspirational and informational articles ("You Can Triumph Over Depression"; "Ten Ways to *Really* Enjoy the Old Testament"; "Witnessing at Work") are available by the dozens in longer, more sophisticated venues every month, so the more active church members may not find them particularly edifying in the newsletter. A single short meditation on the newsletter's theme (if you have one) or any subject of interest will probably be enough for them. Visitors and prospective members, however, appreciate short inspirational and informational articles, particularly when they relate to local or topical issues ("How to Be a Courteous Driver, Even Though 8th Avenue Through Downtown is Blocked Off"; "Is There Life After December 25th?"; "Christian Dating in Los Angeles: Ten Hot Spots"). And in personal evangelism efforts, inspirational/ informational articles are worth their weight in Four Spiritual Laws tracts. Run them in an obvious location on the front cover.

Columns ("Getting into the Word"; "Teen Talk"; "Kids' World") come in two varieties: excellent and terrible. Even professional columnists churn out an occasional bomb and depend on regular, devoted readers to forgive them. Unfortunately, the monthly or biweekly publication schedule of the average church newsletter precludes drumming up much devotion, and of course visitors won't remember any past columns to compare present disasters with. Unless you have access to a syndicated or denomination-wide column, forget it.

The only exception to this rule is the "Pastor's Page" or "Pastor's Pulpit," not a column per se but a chance for the pastoral staff to address the congregation, friends, and the community at large regularly, in print: "What Do We Mean by Stewardship?"; "What's All the Fuss About Pentecost?"; "A Pastoral Postcard from the Interfaith Conference." Pastoral columns provide an excellent soapbox for issues of concern that don't necessarily fit into a Sunday sermon, and they allow visitors and prospective members to get to know the pastor in a leisurely, informal manner. They usually go on the back cover or right inner page (see below). Nearly every church newsletter has a pastoral column, although it is sometimes difficult to get a member of the pastoral staff to submit this month's installment sooner than five minutes before deadline.

Fillers are a broad category that includes quizzes, puzzles, quotations, helpful hints, recipes, anecdotes, and cartoons, along with shorter examples of the previous types of articles. Fillers are vital remedies for the odds and ends of blank space that plague newsletter editors during layout sessions, and they help break up the blocks of text on the newsletter page to provide a necessary variety. A few are inspired, witty, and interesting in their own right. However, including too many will give your newsletter a flimsy, slipshod feel. Use them sparingly: no more than three per page.

Advertisements come in two varieties.

Display ads, usually for businesses and services offered by members of the congregation, can help to pay for some of the expenses of publishing the newsletter as well as take up column-inches of blank space (if blank space is a problem). They can also make the newsletter look cheap and mercenary. Many readers will take offense at advertisements for taco emporiums or legal firms on the same page as an article entitled "Christ is With Us in Our Tragedies." Avoid them.

Classified ads usually occupy the bottom half of the back cover of the newsletter, in inobtrusive small print. They advertise jobs available, jobs wanted, apartments to rent, items for sale, and professional services. While less offensive than display ads and capable of performing a valid service for the congregation, they may still diminish the Christ-centered focus of the newsletter. The unchurched often expect the documents of a Christian church to be "untarnished" by any mention of secular matters, particularly buying and selling. We must avoid giving them the impression that Christianity is nothing but a money-making enterprise. In most cases it's safest to stay away from advertisements altogether (except, of course, advertisements for the newsletter).

Fitting the Newsletter to the Need

A four-page newsletter designed with the primary goal of introducing visitors and prospective members to your church might emphasize local and national religious news, include one or two inspirational articles, and keep events and individual announcements to a minimum. Thus, readers can discover that the church is spiritually alive and aware, an active member of the body of Christ, but they won't be overwhelmed by dozens of unfamiliar names, places, and activities. The final organization might look like this.

Front cover	Left inner page	Right inner page	Back cover
News	Inspirational	Events announcements	Pastor's column
	News	Individual announcements	Inspirational

A four-page newsletter designed as an evangelization tool may emphasize inspirational articles over any other type, and de-emphasize events and individual announcements even more. This format piques the spiritual hunger of the unchurched without giving them the impression that they are eavesdropping on the private correspondence of a country-club church.

Front cover	Left inner page	Right inner page	Back cover
Inspirational	Inspirational	News	Pastor's column
	Events announcements	Inspirational	Individual announcements

Finally, newsletters designed to emphasize the needs of the average church member may devote more space to events and individual announcements and creative pieces, downplay inspirational and informational articles, and put local and denominational religious news on the front cover. Thus, members are made to feel part of the national and international body of Christ, but they can still find out what's happening when they need to know.

Front cover	Left inner page	Right inner page	Back cover
News	Individual announce-ments	Creative work	Pastor's column
	Events announce-ments	Inspirational	Events announce-ments

Of course, every church newsletter fills a variety of needs for a variety of audiences. Your best choice may be to respond to different audiences in different issues (prospective members in May, ordinary members in June, the unchurched in July) and to change the organization of your newsletter accordingly.

Back to the Basics 2

Contrary to what many fledgling editors believe, the church newsletter need not compete with glossies like *Christianity Today* or *Biblical Archaeologist*, with full-page photo spreads, 3000-word feature articles, and interviews with famous theologians. It will not be nearly as permanent, for one thing. If a newsletter article is of exceptional interest, it may be clipped for future reference and discovered by someone's grandnephew in the back of a desk drawer fifty years from now, but usually the entire contents of the newsletter are discarded as soon as the next issue shows up. On the other hand, the newsletter should be more permanent than the one-page typed and mimeographed announcement list, which is usually crammed into a Bible and forgotten or discarded by Sunday afternoon. Visitors and members alike are inundated by pamphlets, tracts, brochures, offering envelopes, Sunday school papers, bulletins, and orders of worship practically every time they walk into the church; therefore, following a few basic guidelines for content, length, page size, frequency of publication, and type of distribution will ensure that the newsletter is perceived as something different, something special.

Content. The newsletter contains information of timeless interest and future events, not a Sunday worship schedule. Lists of hymns, special singers, Bible readings, sermon topics, and complete orders of worship belong in the Sunday bulletin, the "program" of today's service. The church newsletter may contain information about future Sundays (the special singer or evangelist who will visit in June, sermon topics for the next month), as well as a listing of the various church organizations and activities. The most important articles in church newsletters, however, provide information generally unavailable during Sunday morning worship: local, national, and international religious news, personality profiles, surveys, inspirational and informational topics not covered by the pastor's sermon, poetry, anecdotes, and quotations.

Length (number of pages). The newsletter should have more pages than the Sunday bulletin, but fewer than a national religious magazine. Generally speaking, the larger the congregation, the more pages the newsletter will need. The standard size for small churches is a four-page quarto: one sheet of paper folded in half.

Front cover	Inside left	Inside right	Back cover
(Page 1)	(Page 2)	(Page 3)	(Page 4)

If you put text on all four pages, you will have room for between 800 and 1500 words, depending on page size (see below).

Even if your newsletter committee has a budget smaller than the price of the average Stephen King bestseller and less free time than a student in his final year of seminary, do not try to get away with anything shorter. One unfolded piece of paper with text on both sides or with text on a single side, is too short, and the resulting newsletter will be confused with the Sunday bulletin or order of worship—something to be consulted as necessary, not to be read.

A longer, more professional-looking format popular in medium-sized and larger churches is the eight-page quarto. This is nothing more than two four-page quartos, one inserted into the other.

Front cover	Inside left	Inside right	Back cover
(Page 1)	(Page 2)	(Page 7)	(Page 8)

Insert ↓

Outside	Inside left	Inside right	Outside
(Page 3)	(Page 4)	(Page 5)	(Page 6)

An eight-page newsletter allows for enough space to devote the entire front cover to a drawing or photograph of the church, or a different illustration every month depending on the theme, along with the name of the church, the name of the newsletter, and perhaps an identifying logo ("A church with shining lights on Sunday nights"; "More than conquerors"; "A church for all seasons"). The back cover can be devoted to a monthly calendar or the church's unchanging but essential contact information: address and telephone number, parsonage address and telephone number, names of church officers, service times and locations, whom to call in case of emergency. Eight pages are nearly as easy to produce as four pages, requiring only one extra step—stapling the two sheets together before folding. Unfortunately, they also may require up to 2,000 words of text.

A few churches succeed with twelve-page newsletters: three four-page quartos, two inserts, the length of an average suburban or community newspaper. These require up to 3,000 words of text, depending on page size, and as a rule 3,000 words is too long. Edgar Allan Poe advised writers to make no story too long to read in one sitting. In the days before TV sets, video games, and fast-forward buttons, he meant about two hours. The media barrage of contemporary society has decreased the average attention span to about twenty minutes, so no newsletter should take longer than twenty minutes to skim through, an hour to read carefully—at the most.

Page size. Newsletter pages should be larger than those of the Sunday bulletin or order of worship, but smaller than those of a professional magazine. Many churches with low budgets use a page size of 8 1/2" high by 5 1/2" wide—an ordinary 8 1/2" by 11" sheet of paper folded in half. The text can be printed directly from the computer, and the newsletter staff can do all of the photocopying, folding, and stapling themselves, thereby saving a substantial amount when the printshop sends its bill around. Unfortunately, the finished product looks and feels suspiciously like a Sunday bulletin. A more creative option (and more difficult for many word processing systems to format) uses ordinary legal-size paper, 8 1/2" by 14", which when folded in half produces the slightly irregular page size of 8 1/2" high by 7" wide.

Larger churches often go to 11" by 17" sheets of paper folded in half to produce an 8 1/2" wide by 11" high page size. The resulting newsletter is slick, easy to handle, and indisputably professional. Unfortunately, most home and office printers are not set up for 11" by 17" paper, so you must pay a printshop to do the typesetting and printing (you can still do the collating and stapling yourself, for a small savings).

If you have a good relationship with your printshop, a large budget, and an editor who knows what he or she is doing, many other page sizes are feasible, up to 13" wide by 23" high (the size of your hometown newspaper's pages). Extremely large page sizes are not recommended, however, since the pages will then have to be filled with 5,000 or more words of text (depending on the number of pages). You're supposed to inspire and inform readers, not load them down with homework.

Frequency. The newsletter should be published less frequently than Sunday bulletins or orders of worship, but frequently enough to make a positive impact on the congregation. How frequently? The larger the congregation, the more frequent the publication. A weekly publication schedule is too often, since the newsletter will then compete with or replace the Sunday bulletin and give the congregation the impression that the newsletter comes cheaply and easily.

If your church has 500 members, an army of volunteer writers, and a paid professional editor, you may consider a biweekly publication schedule (every other Sunday). Semimonthly, usually the first and third Sunday of the month, can also work. Keep biweekly or semimonthly publication schedules flexible, however; no newsletter staff can be expected to get four or eight pages of text put together during the last two weeks of December, and it's nearly as difficult during the summer, when pulling catfish out of Lake Takawana looks much more promising than coming up with 250 words on "Faith." You should probably limit biweekly or semimonthly newsletters to twenty issues per year, not twenty-four or twenty-six, to exclude periods of activity overload.

Most churches choose a monthly publication schedule, usually as close as possible to the first Sunday of the month. A monthly schedule allows for a regular progression of staff meetings and deadlines, and it is easier for the congregation to remember, reinforcing the idea that the newsletter is a legitimate, dependable venue, not somebody's erratic and soon-to-be-abandoned pet project.

Some churches get by with a new issue every two months, or even quarterly, but newsletters published so infrequently tend to be forgotten by their congregations, and it is next to impossible to drum up support (either in money or volunteer submissions) for a publication everyone has forgotten about. Even in the smallest churches where the editor comprises the entire newsletter staff, aim for a publication schedule of at least once a month. Cut down on the newsletter's page size or number of pages before you cut down on its frequency.

Distribution. Bulletins and orders of worship are distributed during the Sunday morning service, but newsletters are not, both to keep the congregation from reading instead of listening to the sermon and to avoid passing out too many extra copies. Every member of a family sitting in the pew will invariably pick up a copy, and if a mother, a father, and six children happen to be sitting together, you'll be distributing seven more copies than you should. To avoid overdistribution, some churches go as far as to mail their newsletters to every member and then pile the leftover copies on a table in the foyer. This strategy has three dangers. First, anything that shows up in a mailbox unannounced is likely to be tossed onto a stack of "to-be-read" books and magazines and ignored. Second, members often forget that they received a copy of the newsletter in the mail Thursday afternoon, so they pick up another copy Sunday morning. Third, the cost of mailing newsletters to every member is prohibitive.

If a large percentage of your congregation consists of invalids and shut-ins who cannot make it to church every Sunday, then by all means mail your newsletters. In most cases, however, it is more effective and cost efficient to mail the newsletter only to visitors, sister churches and community centers, and anyone else who specifically asks to receive a copy in the mail. Then have a member of the newsletter staff stand in the foyer as the Sunday morning service ends to pass out copies of the newsletter to members of the congregation as they exit. The staff member can keep overdistribution to a minimum by offering one newsletter to each couple or family. For some reason not yet analyzed by psychiatrists, overdistribution is less of a problem after the service than before or during.

Many newsletters fail when their staff members try to figure out how many to distribute. Every month dozens (if not hundreds) of extra copies float about the sanctuary, flutter across the parking lot, and turn up as bookmarks in hymnals, giving the congregation the impression that the newsletter is, well, *cheap*, while at the same time the newsletter budget plummets into the red. While it is better to have too many copies than not enough, most churches print out many more than they will need.

To determine the optimal newsletter run for your church, avoid using the membership roster. If most of your members go to Sunday school or church school, use those statistics instead. Take the total enrollment of all married adult classes and divide by two (one newsletter per couple); if single and married adults attend the same Sunday school classes, divide by 1.5. Add the total enrollment of all single, college and career, and young adult classes, plus about one-third of the high school classes (for those whose parents do not attend church). Most children of junior high age and below will not be interested in the newsletter or will read their parents' copy. The pastor should receive several copies for use in visitation and in counseling prospective members. Also reserve copies for Sunday school teachers, home-evangelism teams, and sister churches, and don't forget at least five file copies. Then add 10 percent to your total for unexpected needs, and you have an estimated print run.

First Baptist has an average attendance of 600 for Sunday morning services, but most of those present are preteens and presumably not spiritually nourished by articles entitled "Let God Manage Your Finances" or "Growing Older Gracefully." Its newsletter staff used Sunday school statistics and determined the optimal press run with this formula:

Adult Sunday school classes, 400 members, mostly married couples, divided by 2	200
College/career class, 75 members, mostly single adults	75
High school classes, 120 members, divided by 3	40
Regular mailing list	20
Newsletter staff, pastoral staff, other office copies	25
Extra 10%	40
TOTAL PRINT RUN	*400*

The Westside Assembly of God also has an average attendance of 300 for Sunday morning services. However, its extensive evangelistic program required sending newsletters home with each of the two hundred Sunday school children bused in from housing projects. Personal evangelization teams required one hundred copies for use in door-to-door canvassing. Its newsletter staff determined the optimal press run with this formula:

Adult Sunday school classes, 200 members, singles and married couples, divided by 1.5	135
High school classes, 120 members, divided by 3	40
Regular mailing list	50
Newsletter staff, pastoral staff, other office copies	25
Extra 10%	25
200 children from bus ministry, each receives one copy	200
100 copies for evangelistic teams	100
TOTAL PRINT RUN	*575*

First Presbyterian had several problems in determining an optimal press run. Membership statistics were not helpful, since they included all baptized infants. Church school records were not helpful, since only a small percentage of those adults who attended Sunday services were actually enrolled in church school classes. Finally they decided to use a list of everyone who contributed to the church during the previous year (ordinarily the entire family contributes as a whole).

They added 20 percent to the list to include those who contributed anonymously as well as those who didn't contribute. The standard 10 percent was added to accommodate visitors.

Adult contributors	200
Plus 20%	40
High school classes, 90 members, divided by 3	30
Regular mailing list	20
Newsletter staff, pastoral staff, other office copies	20
Extra 10%	20
TOTAL PRINT RUN	*330*

If your church has a large-scale evangelization program, you may want to increase the visitors' copies to 20 percent or more. Huge churches with pastoral staffs of twenty or thirty certainly require more office copies than a storefront with a single pastor who drives in from another church on Sunday afternoons. Every church is different, and the optimal print run for yours can best be determined through a few months of careful record keeping.

Is It in the Budget? 3

Actually, you wouldn't need any money for a volunteer editor to input volunteer articles on the church's computer and then print out sixty copies on the church's printer to be collated and stapled by volunteers; but chances are you don't belong to the First Christian Church of Oz. In real life you will run into expenses in six areas.

Expenses

Computer system. This means a real computer, not one of those word processors that are really glorified typewriters. You will need enough RAM (random-access memory, available every time you turn on the computer) to hold the operating system, software package you are using, and the newsletter you are developing with graphics, downloaded clip-art, lines of varying lengths, columns, headers, footers, and font changes, in addition to text. A minimum of 2 megabytes (2,048 kilobytes) is often recommended.

There are two major brands of computers. The Macintosh, manufactured and distributed by the Apple Corporation, is the most versatile. It allows you to grab a block of text and move it anywhere on the screen, to draw any sort of squiggly line you want, and even to paint replicas of art masterpieces, full-color maps of the world, and kittens holding the name of your Children's Choir director in their paws. A dozen innovative software packages—MS-Word, PageMaker, FreeHand, and others—give you many different options for every assignment. A wide variety of fonts in varying sizes and weights, including Hebrew and Greek, are available. Also, what you see on the Macintosh screen is pretty close to what the printed text will look like.

IBM compatible personal computers can also do the job quickly and efficiently, particularly if you don't plan to draw little kittens. You *can* create graphics, lines of various thicknesses, varying fonts, italics, boldface, hundreds of different typographical characters, also including the Greek and Hebrew alphabets, everything except the Mona Lisa. The IBM compatibles allow you to manage files, troubleshoot problems, and easily customize your computer to suit the needs of the newsletter operation.

Both IBM compatibles and Macintoshes, with computer, keyboard, disk drives, and monitor, begin at $1500 to $2000 (1992 prices). A mouse for the IBM compatible or a color monitor for either, will cost an additional few hundred dollars.

Make sure your computer comes with a hard disk, an optional feature that allows storage of programs and text in the computer itself. Ordinary diskettes hold only about 360 kilobytes (K). The high-density kind will hold 1,300 K for IBM compatibles, 400 K to 1,400 K for Macintoshes. Hard disks hold at least 20,000 K (or 20 megabytes). That's enough to accommodate three different software packages, a dozen issues of the newsletter, two years of the minutes of the interfaith outreach committee, the recipe file for the men's Alsatian cooking league, and the complete *Interlinear Greek-Hebrew-English Bible on Disk.*

A printer can represent the major computer-related expense. You can buy run-of-the-mill dot matrix printers (ImageWriters, Epsons) for a few hundred dollars. Don't. Dot matrix printers work just like typewriters: lots of little hammers beat against an ink-soaked ribbon and make impressions on a page. Dot matrix printers may be fine for writing a term paper for an undergraduate political science class, if you don't mind waiting five minutes per page, but they are too slow and too unsophisticated for serious newsletter production. They are usually unable to produce decent-looking clip-art, lines, boxes, diacritical marks (minimal Greek, less Hebrew), point-size changes, or fonts, and the letters will always look like little clusters of dots. Sometimes dealers try to sell you "near-letter quality," a procedure that lets the little hammers bang against the ribbon twice as often. This process takes twice as long, and you can still see the little dots; they are just darker and closer together now.

Laser printers read a page directly from the computer. A laser beam hits a photosensitive drum, which rotates near a reservoir of black powder (the toner used in photocopying). Toner is attracted to the area of the drum hit by the laser and sticks to it, then becomes affixed to the page as the drum continues to roll. What this means is that nothing solid *hits* anything else solid. Not only does the drum last practically forever, the letters it produces look like typesetter's letters. Virtually anything you can design on a page—from a sentence in 5.2-point Times Roman bold italics to the Mona Lisa—can be printed in perfect detail. Laser printers use dots a fraction of the size of those of a dot-matrix printer. An *a* looks like an *a*, whether it's in:

12-point type:	a
or 15-point type:	a

or 80-point type:

Another advantage of laser printers is their speed: eight pages of ordinary text per minute. Three hundred double-sided copies of a four-page newsletter could be printed easily in an hour (though I would recommend photocopying multiple issues). Computer-generated clip-art will increase print time dramatically to five minutes or more per page—but then most dot-matrix printers cannot handle clip-art.

As of this writing, the price of a good laser printer is hovering around $2,000. Prices in the computer world are decreasing all the time, however, and recently laser printers were selling for $1,400 at a discount electronics shop during the Groundhog Day Bargain Blowout.

Word processors can be used effectively for producing a church newsletter. The more recent versions of MS-Word and WordPerfect give you state-of-the-art newsletter and graphics capabilities on either system. If you happen to have an old diskette of WordStar lying around, and you don't mind the eyestrain created by trying to figure out where codes begin and end, it also can be used for newsletters. Page layout software is best for desktop publishing. That software allows the user to make the newsletter's page layout on the computer screen instead of cutting up little pieces of paper and pasting them onto other little pieces of paper. Software packages cost from $100 to $600 depending on power and flexibility. Some software options are summarized in the following table.

Buying a new computer system with computer, monitor, keyboard, disk drives, printer, and software can put

Software type	Macintosh	IBM compatible
Word processing	MS-Word	MS-Word
	WordPerfect	WordPerfect
	MacWrite	WordStar
Graphics	Aldus FreeHand	Corell Draw
	MacDraw	Harvard Graphics
Page layout	Personal Press	Publish It
	PageMaker	Express Publisher
	Quark Xpress	PageMaker
	FrameMaker	Ventura Publisher

a strain of $7,000 or more of one-time start-up expense for a complete computer system, but take heart. There's no need to spend that much on a system you'll be using less than ten hours per month. Having discovered the benefits of using personal computers for keeping track of members, printing out bulletins and correspondence, and even recording sermon notes, most church boards have already authorized the purchase of a shiny new Apple for the church secretary's office or the pastor's study, or both. If not, at least 50 percent of the members of your congregation under the age of thirty-five probably own home computers. Computer time is available free or at minimal expense in many community colleges, universities, photocopy shops, computer stores, and even at the office. With a little ingenuity you will find the expense for computer use negligible.

Office supplies. In the years B.C. (Before the Computer), putting together a newsletter required glue sticks in unending quantities, scissors, tape, blue pens, *lots* of paper, cardboard backing, and probably a layout table. Now you will need nothing more than a few stenographer's notebooks, legal pads, pencils and pens, a good monthly datebook, and a few sheets of 20-pound bond paper on which to print out rough drafts. If you plan on using clip-art, panel cartoons, or photographs, throw in a few glue sticks and pairs of scissors. No more than $10 per month.

Books and magazines. While not essential, a small reference library of dictionaries, writing guides, and basic books on journalistic techniques can come in handy for newsletter staff writers and editors at odd moments. By scouring used bookstores, library book sales, and the basements of board members, you can come up with an adequate collection for between $100 and $300 (see the appendix for suggested titles). Subscriptions to a few professional magazines such as *The Writer, The Editorial Eye,* and *The Christian Writer's Newsletter* can help train the newsletter staff and perhaps spark a few article ideas. You will also want subscriptions to *Christianity Today, The National Christian Reporter*, magazines specializing in quotes and fillers, and your denominational publications, unless the church receives them already. Plan on allowing between $100 and $200 per year for subscriptions to these publications.

Salaries, honoraria, and entertainment. Most newsletters are edited on a volunteer basis, of course, but larger churches desiring longer, more complex newsletters may want to hire a professional editor for between $50 and $200 per month.

All newsletter writing is done on a volunteer basis, with the exception of the very occasional article solicited from the world-famous writer or theologian. In that case, an honorarium is customary: as little as $5 or as much as $200.

Entertainment refers to the pizzas, corn chips, vegetables-and-yogurt-dip, cookies, soft drinks, and coffee consumed by the newsletter staff during monthly or semimonthly brainstorming sessions, and by everyone who shows up for monthly "fold 'n stuff" newsletter collation parties. Depending on the number of volunteers and how many of them decide to pick up doughnuts on the way to the meetings, plan on between $20 and $100 per month.

Printing. Even if you print out all of the copies of the newsletter on your church's laser printer, you will have to pay for the paper sooner or later. Good-quality 20-pound bond paper is available from office supply wholesalers for between $5.00 and $7.00 per ream (more for colored paper and unusual sizes).

Unless you find a great deal or a sympathetic printshop manager, photocopying a double-sided four-page newsletter will cost a minimum of fifteen cents per copy (twice that for an eight-page newsletter, of course). Professional typesetting, photographs, color graphics, and automatic collating-stapling increase the price to as much as seventy-five cents per copy.

For print runs of more than 500 copies, hiring a professional printer is more economical (and will produce better duplication): between three and ten cents per copy for a double-sided four-page newsletter.

Mailing. Obviously you won't be stuffing every copy of the newsletter into an envelope and pasting a stamp on it, but maintaining a mailing list of even 20 percent of your print run at the standard postage rates can still eat up a sizable chunk of the newsletter budget.

If you plan on mailing two hundred or more copies, you can qualify for the U.S. nonprofit bulk rate, which is less than half of standard first-class postage. Your church is no doubt already registered as a nonprofit organization with the IRS, but you have to go through an entirely different (and complicated) procedure with the postal service to register the newsletter. Get an application from the postmaster, and submit it along with copies of your church's constitution, bylaws, financial records, IRS certificate of income tax exemption, and any other helpful documents. You will have to pay an annual fee, sort and bundle the newsletters by zip code, identify each bundle with a postal service color-coded sticker, and deliver the bundles to the post office yourself. It's a lot of work, but worth the time and energy if you've gone into full-scale publication.

For less than two hundred copies the bulk rate does not apply. Simply procure some sponges and rolls of stamps, and add a "mailing" segment to the monthly newsletter production party.

Sample Budgets

Mount Holyoke Witness Church, an outreach mission meeting in the front room of a furniture store, had lots of eager volunteers but very little money to produce 100 copies of a monthly four-page newsletter. Its board of elders approved this annual budget:

Mount Holyoke *Witness*

Computer: Bro. Johnson will do the layout on Macintosh at the Xerox Shack. Costs $2.00/hour, $10/month.	$120.00
Office supplies: none. Newsletter staff members will furnish their own notebooks, etc.	$ 0.00
Books and magazines: none. Newsletter staff members will furnish their own, or use the public library down the street.	$ 0.00
Salaries, honoraria, entertainment: none. Newsletter staff also will furnish their own refreshments.	$ 0.00

Printing: 100 copies, double-sided, collated by hand at the Xerox Shack. 20
cents per copy, $20.00 per month. $240.00
Mailing: none. Church members will
deliver copies to shut-ins during weekly
calling program. Visitors can pick up
theirs at church. $ 0.00

TOTAL ANNUAL BUDGET   *$360.00*

The Full Gospel Tabernacle, membership of 4,000,
with 2,000 more regular attendees, and 4,000 more
adults reached through the weekly *Full Gospel Tabernacle Today* television broadcast, was interested in producing a slick eight-page newsletter to be distributed
during street-corner and door-to-door evangelization
ministries and mailed to all visitors and inquirers. Its
board approved a considerably larger budget.

Full Gospel Tabernacle *Faith Beacon*

Computer: newsletter editor will do the
layout on the Macintosh in the church
office. $ 0.00
Office supplies: newsletter staff will receive its own shelf in the supply closet
in the church office, $10 per month. $ 120.00
Books and magazines: newsletter staff
will receive subscriptions to *Christianity Today, The Editorial Eye, The Christian Writer's Newsletter,* and *The Pentecostal Herald*. $ 139.00
Salaries, honoraria, entertainment: paid
professional editor, $100 per month.
$50 per month for newsletter staff
refreshments. $1800.00

Printing: Bro. Miller of Miller's Printing
will give the church a special discount
on 3,000 copies—15¢ each, $450 per
month. $5400.00

Mailing: monthly mailing to 500 inquirers from the television program, 500
visitors, and 500 others. 1,500 copies,
nonprofit rate @ 13.5¢, $202.50 per
month. $2430.00

TOTAL ANNUAL BUDGET   *$9889.00*

Your church probably fits somewhere between these
two extremes of church size and financial solvency. If
you want to print 200 copies of an eight-page monthly
newsletter with a minimum of color illustrations and
photographs, mail 20 copies every month, and have a
few hundred dollars left over to provide refreshments
for monthly newsletter-collating parties, you should
probably set aside at least $1,200 per year—50¢ total
per copy. Producing a professional-quality newsletter
can cost considerably more, but it rarely costs less.

The Newsletter Staff   4

The ideal newsletter staff consists of an editor, five or more regular staff writers, a bevy of occasional volunteer contributors, and lots of volunteers eager to do the messy jobs such as inputting copy and delivering diskettes to the printer. More common in most churches is the nonideal staff, consisting of an editor, two regular staff writers, and as many volunteers as a two-minute speech during Sunday announcements a week before publication can drum up. The newsletter's ministry depends on the enthusiasm, talent, and commitment of its staff, so it is vital that each staff member be carefully chosen.

Personnel

The editor. Unless the entire church board has just moved to Florida with the entire pastoral staff, and the two or three members who always volunteer for everything are out sick, the senior pastor should never serve as the newsletter editor. The church will perceive the resulting newsletter as little more than an extension of the Sunday morning sermon, and they will probably be right. If your newsletter is to perform an effective ministry, its editor should have few other congregational responsibilities. No one can prepare two sermons a week, counsel church members, chair miscellaneous committees, solve miscellaneous disputes, and still expect to devote a good five hours per week to editing the newsletter.

The assistant pastor, pastor's wife, or ministerial intern often gets stuck with the job of editing the newsletter, but it is better to inquire among members of the congregation for a freelance writer, newspaper editor, journalist, English teacher, technical writer, even a word processor or secretary—anyone who has a familiarity with both editorial techniques and computer software. A degree in English or journalism is a plus, as is some sort of editorial experience (magazines, community newspapers, other newsletters), but a soon-to-be editor can learn the basics in a few hours by talking to newsletter editors from other churches or dropping by the public library, or by reading this book. Most community colleges offer low-cost, low-pressure courses in desktop publishing, writing nonfiction, journalism, even newsletter editing. In fact, it wouldn't be a bad idea to suggest that the entire newsletter staff register for one of these courses.

If you are planning on a long newsletter (more than eight pages) or an especially complex layout (cartoons, color photographs, many font sizes and styles), you may want to consider hiring a professional newsletter editor. Check the *Literary Market Place*, classified and display ads in *The Writer*, your denominational publications, and church and community bulletin boards for freelance writers who specialize in church newsletters.

A professional editor is usually hired by the church board or publications committee on the basis of her or his resumé, writing samples, references, and (*very* important) samples of previous newsletters. He or she works on a month-to-month basis; thirty days' notice is customary for either the editor or the board to terminate the relationship. The salary (determined in advance) is between $50 and $200 per month, depending on the size and complexity of the requested newsletter. Since many professionals work on five or more newsletters at the same time, you should not insist that the editor join your congregation or even attend regularly. The editor will need a sense of your church's character and special needs, however, so you may request attendance at a few services at the beginning of the relationship and thereafter whenever convenient.

It is important to clarify the editor's responsibilities before accosting the congregation for volunteers or trotting down to the library to check out the *Literary Market Place*. In most cases, the editor is responsible for moderating staff meetings, passing out the writing assignments, editing the articles for grammar and style, and making the final decisions about the newsletter's content and layout. She or he will also keep track of supplies and expenses; address the church board, publications committee, or congregation as a whole when necessary; train other staff members in computer, writing, and interviewing skills; maintain the relationship with the printer; and answer any inquiries about the newsletter from members of the congregation or the outside community. This may seem like a lot of work, but under most circumstances it doesn't take more than twenty hours per month.

If you hire a professional editor from outside the congregation, someone else (probably one of the staff writers) will need to take care of the newsletter's publicity, that is, get up in front of the congregation during the announcements to solicit contributions, visit Sunday school classes and men's prayer breakfasts, affix posters to the bulletin board in the fellowship hall, and generally make the newsletter's presence known to the congregation.

In the smallest or busiest congregations, the newsletter editor may inherit the responsibility for all of the publicity, writing, inputting, layout, photocopying, collating, folding, and stapling, as well as printing out mailing labels, affixing them to twenty copies, driving them to the post office, and hand-delivering another twenty copies to a nursing home thirty miles away. These jobs can easily take up twenty additional hours, for a total of forty hours per month (sometimes all during the same week)—beyond the capacity of all but the most zealous workaholic. In such a situation, the newsletter editor should exercise all possible managerial, supervisory, and motivational power to drum up an enthusiastic and dedicated newsletter staff.

Staff writers. Events announcements and individual announcements, to be compiled by the editor or a volunteer, usually occupy a total of about two pages. Short articles borrowed from uncopyrighted denominational publications, other church newsletters, and secular news sources ordinarily take up about a page. That leaves one page of a four-page quarto and five pages of an eight-page quarto to be filled every month. It doesn't sound like much until the two blank pages are still staring out of your computer screen at two A.M. the morning *after* your printer's deadline. Effective church newsletters depend upon staff writers even more than editors.

Most church newsletters are open to any freelance effort, submitted by any church member, visitor, or interested friend at any time of the day or night; but if you want to produce a newsletter that doesn't look slapped together at the last minute, you will need firm commitments from two or more staff writers to attend regular meetings, accept writing assignments, and, most importantly, produce. Fortunately, imaginative writing has become one of the most popular pastimes of the twentieth century. There are some two hundred college-level creative writing programs in the United States, and more opportunities to study college journalism than algebra. Virtually every church can boast its share of would-be epic poets, Pulitzer prize–winning journalists, Nobel prize–winning novelists, diarists, columnists, and essayists. The trick is to find them, get them motivated, and *keep* them motivated.

Start out with the usual strategy of standing in front of the congregation and asking if anyone would like to write for the newsletter; but don't stop there. Visit Sunday school classes, youth groups, singles groups, the choir, any church organization. Pass out samples of the proposed newsletter, prepared specifically for recruitment purposes. Keep an ongoing notice on the church bulletin board. Put up a box for article ideas outside the newsletter office, with paper and pens available. Publicize and hold a workshop in writing and layout skills for prospective newsletter writers, and give free copies of Strunk and White's *Elements of Style* or *The Associated Press Stylebook and Libel Manual* to everyone who participates.

Standards of selection for staff writers differ considerably from those for the selection of editors. While the newsletter editor should be free from other time-consuming commitments in the church, staff writers should be as active and involved as possible (to give them more things to write about). While a minimal command of the English language would be nice, and every newsletter editor dreams of a staff of published professional writers, the dependability and enthusiasm of staff writers are much more important than writing talent. It is a good idea, however, to request would-be staff writers to submit two or three sample articles.

They will not be used to weed out the poor writers, just to weed out those who aren't interested enough to actually submit something.

The staff writer is responsible for attending all staff meetings, suggesting article ideas, writing one or more articles totaling between 100 and 500 words per month, and participating in decisions regarding the newsletter content and layout. He or she should also share in the responsibility for inputting and printing the newsletter text, photocopying (or delivery to the printshop), collating, stapling, and distribution. Experienced writers will be able to take care of all newsletter responsibilities in ten hours per month; less experienced writers may require twenty.

Good, dependable staff writers are hard to find, and harder to keep; the best ones are being swallowed up by other church organizations or turning into professional freelancers. It is vital, therefore, that the editor keep staff writers happy by announcing meetings and deadlines long in advance (preferably a month), including a byline for any article a staff writer produces over a paragraph in length, and publishing something by each staff writer in each issue of the newsletter. Sometimes the editor must play the role of the writing instructor by offering individual critiques and advice, suggesting writing courses and conferences and exercises, and giving short speeches on such writing basics as wordiness, vagueness, and diction. Sometimes the editor must act as mentor or coach. Most often, however, the editor must be a colleague. The church newsletter should be considered a team effort, even if the editor is a professional journalist and the staff writers are nonprofessionals.

Staff assistants. Individuals too timid to commit themselves to being staff writers may be interested in contributing to the newsletter team by helping to input articles (professional secretaries and word processors can work wonders in this regard), photocopy, deliver the camera-ready copy to the printshop, collate, staple, stamp, and distribute. These minor but essential activities can be relegated to any volunteer who happens to show up for a monthly "newsletter party"—a risky business at best. Of course, the newsletter editor and staff writers can (and usually do) take care of these jobs themselves; but a few dependable nonwriters can lower stress levels immeasurably toward the end of the month.

The newsletter editor ordinarily has the final vote in all staff assignments. Usually the same staff writer or staff assistant takes responsibility for the same task every month. For example, you might have a staff assistant to do each of the following: input, deliver to and pick up from the printer, affix mailing labels, deliver copies to the post office, with all staff helping to collate and staple.

However, staff members often prefer to switch responsibilities from issue to issue. Unfortunately, this requires more managerial ability from the editor. She or he must determine the work schedule, remind people of their assignments, and make sure the assignments get done. It helps to chart the duties on a twelve-month basis in advance. In the end, it probably takes more time, energy, and memory cells, but it results in a happier staff.

Occasional contributors and volunteers. The newsletter belongs to the entire congregation, and the newsletter staff should do its best to get as many people involved as possible. A good way to start is to announce the theme of this month's newsletter (if any) during one or two Sunday morning services, and solicit contributions. But don't stop there. If the youth group has just returned from a trip to Chicago, don't be satisfied with an interview; ask the director of the youth group to write an article. If Sam Rozinsky has just been admitted to the doctoral program in homiletics at Union Theological Seminary, don't just report on the event; ask him for a write-up. Offer workshops on "How to Write Religious Articles," open to the entire church and the outside community. Sit in on Sunday school classes, choir practice, the Wednesday night prayer league, and the missionary society. Ask to follow the pastor or assistant pastor on his daily routine. The more visible the newsletter staff, the more support the newsletter will receive.

Keeping to the Schedule

Staff meetings. A smoothly running newsletter requires staff meetings at regular intervals, usually every week or every two weeks, to set a tone of continuity. Tuesdays or Thursdays work best; avoid Monday and Friday nights as if they were Christmas Eve. And make every effort to end the staff meetings before *The Tonight Show*. The all-night brainstorming sessions that you remember fondly from college are fun only in retrospect. Adults, particularly those with children and jobs, like to be home at a decent hour.

Following a monthly publication schedule, you can devote one session to planning the theme for the month and brainstorming article ideas, one session to gathering the articles and planning the newsletter's layout, and another session to any necessary collating, stapling, mailing, and distribution. Your monthly schedule might look like this:

April Newsletter Schedule

MON   1
TUES   2

WED	3	Newsletter meeting: April newsletter collated and stapled.
THU	4	Copies to be mailed delivered to post office.
FRI	5	
SAT	6	
SUN	7	Remaining copies of April newsletter distributed after morning service.
MON	8	
TUES	9	
WED	10	Newsletter meeting: May newsletter planned. Theme? Articles suggested and assigned.
THU	11	
FRI	12	
SAT	13	
SUN	14	During morning service, newsletter editor announces the May theme to the congregation and solicits contributions.
MON	15	
TUES	16	
WED	17	Newsletter meeting: progress report on assigned articles. Additional suggestions and contributions.
THU	18	
FRI	19	
SAT	20	
SUN	21	
MON	22	Deadline for all submissions.
TUES	23	
WED	24	Newsletter meeting: decisions on contents and layout of May newsletter made. Decisions on cover art, clip art, cartoons. Editor or volunteer to do input, layout, printing, and photocopying by next meeting.

THU	25	
FRI	26	
SAT	27	
SUN	28	
MON	29	
TUES	30	
WED	1	MAY. Newsletter meeting: May newsletter collated and stapled.

If you need to use a printshop instead of photocopying, collating, and stapling the newsletter yourself, count on at least a week between delivery and pickup. The submission deadline, consequently, should be a week earlier.

April Newsletter Schedule

MON	1	
TUES	2	
WED	3	Editor picks up April newsletter at the printer. Newsletter meeting: examination of newsletter to make sure it is satisfactory. May newsletter planned. Theme? Articles suggested and assigned.
THU	4	Copies to be mailed delivered to post office.
FRI	5	
SAT	6	
SUN	7	Remaining copies of April newsletter distributed after morning service. Newsletter editor announces the May theme and solicits contributions.
MON	8	
TUES	9	

WED	10	Newsletter meeting: progress report on assigned articles. Additional suggestions and contributions.
THU	11	
FRI	12	
SAT	13	
SUN	14	
MON	15	Deadline for all submissions.
TUES	16	
WED	17	Newsletter meeting: decisions on contents and layout of May newsletter made. Decisions on cover art, clip art, cartoons. Editor or volunteer to do input and layout by next meeting.
THU	18	
FRI	19	
SAT	20	
SUN	21	
MON	22	
TUES	23	
WED	24	Newsletter meeting: staff reviews final layout. Editor drops off text at the printshop.
THU	25	
FRI	26	
SAT	27	
SUN	28	
MON	29	
TUES	30	
WED	1	MAY. Editor picks up May newsletter at the printshop.

Deadlines. The above sample schedules give staff writers less than two weeks between receiving their assignments and the deadline: certainly not enough time for a staff writer at *The New York Times* or *Cosmopolitan*. But the church newsletter does not pretend to be *The New York Times* or *Cosmopolitan*, or, for that matter, the *Sagebrush County Times-Gazette*. Most newsletter articles are between 50 and 300 words long, which all but the least experienced writers can bang out in an hour. Most newsletter articles do not require extensive preparation or research: a single fifteen-minute interview with the youth pastor during the Sunday morning fellowship hour, a moment with *Cruden's Compact Concordance* to make sure John 14:1–2 is quoted correctly. The editor should face no insurmountable problems in setting deadlines; it might be wise, however, to set the deadlines a few days before the articles are actually needed, to accommodate those staff writers who stumble in twenty hours late, panting and wheezing, holding out handwritten copy on the back of an envelope. In staff meetings, emphasize that setting and meeting deadlines is essential to produce an effective, professional-looking newsletter.

If staff writers consistently miss deadlines, that's all right, too. They are volunteers, they all have day jobs, this isn't *The New York Times*, and no one is going to leave the church in a huff if the newsletter shows up on the *second* Sunday of the month once in a while.

Getting the Scoop 5

Church newsletter articles are easy to write. Just follow the advice Lewis Carroll gives in *Through the Looking Glass*: "Start at the beginning. Then go on until you come to the end. Then stop." The key word is *stop*. Most new writers go on far too long.

What Goes in It

You can buy books on how to construct articles with clever catch phrases, stunning beginning paragraphs, precise logical development, and intriguing conclusions (see appendix for suggestions). Event announcements and individual announcements do not require such elegance, however. An article about an upcoming chili cook-off can be input onto the computer screen with little more than those first-day-of-high-school-journalism standbys, the five Ws and one H:

Who is doing (did) it?
What is (was) it?
Where and *when* is it happening (did it happen)?
Why should I go (should I have gone)?
How can I sign up?

The Biblical Languages, Archaeology, and History Society (BLAHS) will host its annual chili cook-off in the church parking lot on Saturday, June 8, from 10:00 A.M. to 3:00 P.M. Soft drinks and antacids will be provided, and prizes will be awarded for the best chili in four categories (most original, hottest, tastiest, best consistency). Sign up in the church office, or see Zador Howell, president.

One paragraph, three sentences, 67 words.

Even a more complicated event announcement or individual announcement does not require hours of agonizing before the computer screen. Just repeat the pattern twice, in two paragraphs: once for what's happening now, then again for background information.

The church board announces the call of Reverend Wheelwright McThurow to the office of senior minister beginning in August 1992. Many members of the congregation will recall that Rev. McThurow visited our church last March, when he preached on "The Influence of the Qumran Eschatological Writings on Nascent Pauline Theology."

Rev. McThurow comes to us from the Enid, Oklahoma, First Faith Church, where he served as youth pastor for five years. He studied at Barter College (Kenosha, Wisconsin) and Tuscaloosa Theological Seminary, and he has served on the editorial board of *Modern Homiletics* magazine. He will be accompanied by his wife, Sarah Esther, and his fifteen-year-old son, Mark.

A little over a hundred words (112, to be exact).

Inspirational/informational and news articles are usually longer than individual or events announcements—100 to 300 words or more—and they require a more complex structure. Not much more complex, though.

Opening hook. The first sentence of the article sometimes encompasses the standard five Ws and an H, but more frequently it is a short, intriguing sentence that sets the tone of the piece and compels the reader to read on: "Why is it that when the phone rings at 2:00 A.M. it's never good news?"; "You don't have to be a professional theologian to read the minor prophets"; "Easter and the Jewish Passover rarely fall on the same weekend, but this year they did, and Rev. Tom Walters and Rabbi Jacob Edelman thought they'd do something about it." Notice that none of these sentences is going to be nominated for a Pulitzer prize: the opening hook of a church newsletter article should be interesting, intriguing, but not Edward R. Murrow.

Beginning. The rest of the opening paragraph consists of about 50 words of names, dates, places. Who was on the phone? What good are the minor prophets? What did Rev. Walters and Rabbi Edelman do to commemorate Easter and Passover?

Middle. The middle paragraphs, 50 to 200 words, develop the opening paragraph, using some of the same techniques you learned in high school English: description ("The emergency room looked pale and deserted, somehow unreal in the Tuesday morning twilight."); definition ("The Seder is the Passover meal, observed by millions of Jews all over the world in celebration of their liberation from bondage in Egypt."); comparison-contrast ("While Jews abandoned the custom of lying down for the Passover Seder hundreds of years ago, Christians recreating the Last Supper invariably go in for couches."); and classification ("Few people realize that there are three types of prophets: pre-exile, exile, and post-exile."). You may also include background research, quotations from interviews, and personal observations.

Ending. The closing paragraph, 10 to 50 words, recapitulates the article in a catchy (or not catchy, if you're tired) sentence or two. Often it includes a number to call for further information. Sometimes, rarely effectively, it ends with an exclamation point ("This celebration was the best ever!").

But how do you find the facts for these articles? Hearsay, rumor, or "just knowing" is not sufficient. Even listening to the oral announcements that form a standby of the Sunday morning service will give you an incomplete and often inaccurate version of the event. Unless you happen to be the chair of the decide-on-the-color-of-the-new-hymnals committee, your article on the new mauve hymnals will require at least one interview. Fifteen minutes with an individual in authority can easily be transformed into an event or individual announcement of up to 200 words; a half-hour interview can be transformed into a 500-word profile or news feature.

How to Interview

Many inexperienced newsletter writers and editors have difficulty with interviews, particularly since most of the time they are talking to personal friends and acquaintances. The interview quickly devolves into a discussion of last Saturday's potluck dinner, preschoolers' escapades, and job prospects. While interviewers should strive to put their subjects at ease and maintain a courteous, friendly attitude, it is important that they treat interviews with friends and church acquaintances as business meetings, not personal visits.

In interviews with church leaders, particularly those from outside the local church, the opposite is frequently a problem. The interviewer becomes cold, even abrasive, perhaps trying to reflect Barbara Walters grilling Manuel Noriega, not one member of the Christian community receiving information from another. Approaching the interview as an opportunity to make an interesting new acquaintance may minimize this problem.

Set up the interview several days in advance. No pastor likes to be importuned as he walks back to his office at 12:35 Sunday afternoon, exhausted after announcements, three songs, two prayers, a confirmation, a thirty-minute sermon, and an altar call. Although most of the people you might want to interview are available before church Sunday morning, the flurry and confusion of putting together a church service makes this a rather poor time to approach them. Setting up the interview in advance will give both you and your subject time to prepare.

Prepare a list of questions in advance. Nothing is more embarrassing than to be sitting across from an interview subject who is smiling expectantly—and no question presents itself. The five Ws and one H should be on any list of interview questions, of course, along-with any other questions you think a reader might want to know. You needn't stick to the list; other questions will certainly arise during the course of the interview. However, keeping the list handy will ensure that the most important questions are asked and answered.

Choose a quiet, private place to hold the interview. Not the sanctuary foyer, where people are milling about, greeting each other, criticizing the pastor's new suit, and asking "So, what's going on?" A secluded corner of the fellowship hall is fine. Better is the pastor's office (if you're interviewing the pastor), the newsletter office, a deserted Sunday school classroom, or the interviewee's home (if it seems proper: Men should not interview single women at home, and vice versa).

Stick to the topic of the interview. Particularly with personal friends it is difficult to avoid veering off to spouses, children, careers, dogs. Keep your mind and questions on the topic, and if the interviewee starts meandering, simply say, "That's fascinating, and I'd love to discuss it with you later. But for now . . ." and go on to the next question on your list.

Also avoid interjecting your own opinions. You may ask questions, of course, and you may voice short agreements or disagreements with the interviewee's opinions, but do not turn the interview into a discussion. The purpose of the interview is not to exchange ideas but to gather information.

Take only a few short, specific notes. Constant scribbling puts off most interviewees, and tape recorders are unnecessary for interviews under half an hour long. Chances are you will remember everything important for hours after the interview anyway, so write down only the tiny but essential details that you might get confused about later: Is the meeting at 7:30 or 8:00? Will the new baptismal font cost $300 or $3000? Is it Horace *T.* or Horace *R.* Blumengardener?

Input your article as soon as possible after the interview, preferably within a few hours, certainly the same day. (For this reason, if you don't want to work on the computer on Sunday, don't conduct the interview on Sunday.) Not only will your memory still be fresh and reliable if you input the article quickly, but you'll have time to print out a copy for the interviewee to check before your editing, layout, and publication. It's rather embarrassing to misspell the new pastor's name, or to indicate that Mr. and Mrs. Birdsall are celebrating their *fiftieth* not their *fifth* anniversary, on copy that no one but the parties involved can really correct.

For every sort of article except individual and events announcements and profiles of individuals in the congregation, you will need more than interviews. At some point you will have to evoke the second mainstay of article writing: research.

How to Research an Article

Use Reference Books. Most research is little more than checking facts: refreshing your memory about when the Book of Nahum was written, how many theses Luther nailed to the Wittenberg door, or how *shekinah* is spelled. For fact checking you will need nothing but your brain and a few basic reference books. Do not depend on the public library or the church library; most of us do our writing at home, in front of a personal computer in the bedroom or on a yellow legal pad at the kitchen table, at odd hours when it's inconvenient or impossible to get to the library. Besides, you can't keep breaking your train of thought every five minutes to put on your coat and drive across town to look up John Wesley's birthdate.

A good **dictionary** (not necessarily the one you got in college). *Webster's New World Dictionary*, the second college edition (Cleveland: New World Dictionaries, 1984) is the standard; *Webster's Third New International Dictionary of the English Language* (Springfield, Mass.: Merriam, 1981) is bulkier, maybe too bulky for everyday use. Many computer word processing programs come with dictionaries, but they are not nearly complete enough.

A **thesaurus** for finding words that get caught somewhere between your left brain and your cerebral cortex. *Roget's International Thesaurus*, 4th edition (New York: HarperCollins, 1977) should be supplemented by the alphabetical *Merriam-Webster Thesaurus* (Springfield, Mass.: Merriam, 1989). Many computer word processing programs come with thesauruses, but like the built-in dictionaries, they are not complete enough.

An **almanac** for looking up secular statistics, names, and dates. Houghton Mifflin's *Information Please Almanac* and the *World Almanac and Book of Facts* (World Almanac, Inc.) both come out every year. It's not essential to buy every new version, however; statistics don't change that much, and chances are you're not going to be all that interested in who won the Oscars or the American League pennant last year. Replace your copy every two or three years.

An **encyclopedia**. The Britannicas and World Books aren't as useful as you might think; by the time you finish reading a thirty-page article on Beethoven or Carthage or steam engines, you will have forgotten what you wanted to know. On the other hand, a one-volume encyclopedia, such as *The Concise Columbia Encyclopedia*, 2d ed. (New York: Columbia University Press, 1989) will tell you when Alain-Fournier wrote *The Wanderer* and the 1980 population of Hiroshima quickly and easily.

Bibles: the King James Version, the Revised Standard Version, the New International Version, and the New American Standard Bible, for starters.

A **concordance**. *Cruden's Complete Concordance* (Zondervan), or *Strong's Concordance* (Nelson).

Bible commentaries, **handbooks**, and **dictionaries**. Depending on your denomination, you may choose the *New Bible Dictionary* (Tyndale), *Evangelical Commentary of the Bible* (Baker), *Evangelical Dictionary of the Bible* (Baker), or any of a dozen others.

For more extensive research, particularly for articles with a historical, biographical, or topical basis, you will need to use your church and denominational libraries, the public library, or local college and university libraries. If you have a modem you can often access area library catalogs through the ORION system. A number of on-line databases are also available. See the appendix for suggested books, periodicals, and other resources.

Plan out your research in advance. If you are writing on a topic of current interest ("How Christians Can Fight Job Stress"), you might try the *Reader's Guide to Periodical Literature;* for a topic of timeless interest ("Five Ways to Keep Your Kids in Sunday School"), the *Reader's Guide* will be practically worthless. Will your research require secular or religious sources? Primarily books, magazines, or newspapers? After researching a few articles, most writers have the layout of their local library pretty much memorized; which section of the library will you be using? Organization will keep you from time-consuming distractions and dead ends.

Take careful notes. Any name, place, date, or other vital piece of information you leave out will require a new trip to the library. Many writers make a habit of photocopying essential articles and pages of reference books (keeping their budgets and copyright laws in mind). It may be a good idea to write out the information you need on index cards in advance, to be sure that you won't leave the library without filling it in.

An article on Martin Luther's Wittenberg door experience, for instance, would require considerable his-

torical and theological research. The card may look like
this before the library visit:

> Article: You Don't Have to Be Lutheran:
>   The Wittenberg Door for Today's Christian
> Luther:
> Date of birth:
> Date of death:
> Studied:
> Wittenberg door date:
> Location of Wittenberg:
> Theses examples:
>   1.
>   2.
> Importance of the event:
> Luther's important writings:
> Important doctrines:
> Important Lutheran theologians:
> Luther's importance for all Christians:
> Sources consulted:

Of course, you may not need all of this information
for the article, but it will be there, just in case.

An article based primarily on personal experiences
or interviews with church members will require less
library research.

> Article: Laid Off!
>   The Christian Response to the Pink Slip
> Number of people laid off in U.S. every year:
> Percentage of work force:
> Psychological/emotional difficulties involved:

Advice of secular psychologists, job placement counselors:

1.

2.

Advice of Christian psychologists, counselors, pastors:

1.

2.

Relevant Scripture:

Sources consulted:

Do not over research. It would be pointless and time-consuming to track down all of the references on "Depression" in the *Readers Guide to Periodical Literature* for a 500-word newsletter article on "Christian Depression," or to list all of the books written on the Dead Sea Scrolls within the last fifty years for an article on "What the Dead Sea Scrolls Mean to Christians Today." If a topic is interesting, a writer can often spend hours looking up more and more information, more than she or he can ever hope to use, out of the sheer love of learning. Learning is certainly important, but not when you have a five o'clock deadline and twelve other errands to run. An effective rule (which you may break as often as necessary) is one reference book, magazine article, or newspaper article for every hundred words. A 500-word article, therefore, should require no more than five references.

Write your article as soon after the research as possible, preferably within a few hours. Just as in interviewing, research provides the bare bones of an article that need to be fleshed out while the information is fresh in your mind. Your notes may seem perfectly clear now, but in a few days they may be as incomprehensible as Minoan Linear-B. Also, writing the article as soon as possible will give you a chance to see if you left out any vital information, or if you will need to return to the library for additional research before the deadline.

Stealing Somebody Else's Stuff

Not exactly—but thousands of news stories that you cannot get your hands on are being researched and written every day by an army of freelance writers (called stringers) and made available for reprint by all local newspapers, including church newsletters. The United Press International (UPI) and the Associated Press (AP) provide general news (infrequently of a religious nature) for a rather expensive subscription fee, but a number of more economical news services are oriented toward the religious markets: the National Council of Christians and Jews News Service, the Evangelical Press Association News Service, the Ecumenical Council News Service, and others (check appendix for addresses). Stories received from a service may be reprinted in full, or they may be cut and edited to meet the needs of your particular congregation.

Copyright Laws: What You Can Print

The good news is that your newsletter article is copyrighted. You don't need to fill out any forms, pay any fees, send any copies to the Library of Congress. Beginning January 1, 1978, every written work created in the United States, whether published or not, is copyrighted.

The bad news is that everything you write, even if you don't intend it for publication—memos, letters, diaries, laundry lists, cute sayings on the bottom of get-well cards—everything is copyrighted while you are alive and then for fifty years after your death. If you scribble a note to your grandson to congratulate him on his high-school graduation, and forty-nine years after your death a future historian publishes it in his monumental *Congratulatory and Thank-You Notes of the American 1990s*, your great-great grandson can sue him.

Since everything is copyrighted, what *can* you print in your newsletter?

All staff-written and volunteer submissions, provided they have not been published elsewhere before (usually not a problem; writers will rarely publish articles in *People Magazine* and then try to submit them to the *First Methodist Church Newsletter*).

Quotations from the Bible, classic authors (including Shakespeare and everybody from ancient Greece and Rome) and authors who have been dead more than fifty years (John Wesley, Dwight L. Moody, Dickens, Tennyson).

Excerpts from books of fillers, anecdotes, cartoons, and sermon illustrations specifically published for public speakers, pastors, journalists, or newsletter writers. Check the title page if you're not sure. Those books that do not want you to excerpt them for your newsletter will include a notice on the back of the title page, such as: "All rights reserved. No part of this work may be reproduced or transmitted in any form or by any means, electronic or mechanical, including photocopying and recording, or by any information storage or retrieval system, except as may be expressly permitted by the 1976 Copyright Act or in writing from the publisher."

Articles from limited-circulation newsletters, such as the *Riverside Baptist Church Monthly* or *Olivet*

Methodist Manna, provided that they do not include a little notice prohibiting reproduction. Articles from a news service: It's customary to mention the news service in the byline of the article: "Resurgence of Interest in Learning Ugaritic Noted in Nation's Theological Schools (Associated Church Press)." Articles from some denominational and interdenominational magazines: Some denominational publications may be excerpted by members of the denomination only, others are open to everyone, and still others reserve all rights. Check the title page or your denominational headquarters to make sure.

You will need to get written permission to publish articles or substantial sections of articles from most national religious and secular magazines (a standard release form is available for this purpose). While permission is usually not a problem, the process can take between six weeks and six months, so don't call *The Christian Single Digest* the day before the December issue deadline to see if you can reprint their article on "Six Ways to Survive Christmas Away from Home." And don't try to publish an article from a national magazine without getting permission. Chances are no one will notice, but it's unprofessional and immoral.

Regardless of the source, it is customary to include a brief byline for every article, where the author's name would usually go: "From the Evangelical Press Association"; "Reprinted from the Southside Presbyterian Church *Acolyte*"; "From *The Baptist Voice*, June 1990. Used by permission."

Christmas, Easter, Labor Day . . . 6

Choosing Themes

Planning your newsletter around a holiday, seasonal, or other theme has some distinct advantages. Themes create an immediate interest. Instead of a melange of articles on every topic under the sun, readers know that they can look forward to five articles on "Palm Sunday" or "The Christian Home." A call during the Sunday morning service for articles on "Christ in the Workplace" will usually receive a much greater response than a call for articles on "any topic"; it's easier to get volunteers thinking and writing about something specific.

It's also easier to create a logical plan of organization for a newsletter when you've decided on the theme in advance. Mother's Day? An article idea on mothers past, present, and future should pop up effortlessly enough; add an interview with the oldest mother in the church, a reflection on Mary the mother of Jesus or Hannah the mother of Samuel, "A Working Mother's Prayer," and a few fillers, and your newsletter is virtually complete. Veteran's Day? Solicit a firsthand reflection from a high school senior about to join the Marines, or a veteran just back from four years in the Navy; assign articles on the "whole armor of God" in Ephesians and how the hymn "Onward, Christian Soldiers" came to be written; consider (and reject) the old chestnut about the soldier saved from an enemy bullet by the New Testament in his front pocket; and voila!

Unfortunately, themes also have distinct disadvantages. If you force every article in the newsletter to conform to a restrictive theme, your audience will become bored rather quickly. Also, some themes are so overworked that it's difficult to find articles of sufficient interest. Assign articles on "School Daze" in August, or "Christmas" the second week of December, and you're sure to incite mutiny in the ranks of the newsletter staff writers.

To keep a theme from overwhelming and/or boring the intended audience, follow two old rules of style you probably learned in freshman composition but which remain valid for any sort of writing project: 1) *Suggest* rather than state; and 2) Variety is the spice of life.

Alternate types of themes. Themes come in three varieties: holiday related ("Father's Day"; "Martin Luther King's Birthday"; "Memorial Day"); seasonal but not holiday related ("John Wesley's Birthday"; "The Day Our Church Was Founded"; "Back to School"); and timeless ("Christian Stewardship"; "The Great Commission"; "Getting to Know Your Pastoral Staff"). Try to use all three types at some point during the fiscal year. If you put together an exciting, inspiring newsletter on the theme "Memorial Day" in May, it will take an act of God to garner enthusiasm for the theme "Flag Day" in June or "Independence Day" in July. "Easter" in April probably precludes a newsletter theme of "Pentecost" in May; "Christian Stewardship" in June should not be followed by "Using Your Talents" in July.

Alternate article types. Instead of planning *every* article around the newsletter's theme, alternate between thematic and nonthematic articles. Intersplice two articles on "Easter" with a filler about pew-warming churchgoers. If you have an article, a filler, and a piece of clipart on "Independence Day," use them on the same page as an article about the youth choir's upcoming visit to the district talent competition in Kenosha, Wisconsin.

Use theme-related graphic devices sparingly. A few judiciously placed oak leaves and acorns can suggest autumn; trees shedding leaves in bales, squirrels grinning from piles of acorns, and family members in pilgrim hats praying around a Thanksgiving table quickly become abrasive. Newsletters seem particularly susceptible to overuse of graphics around Christmastime; practically every page is bordered by stars, shepherds on hillsides, donkeys staring up from mangers, even some incongruous wrapped presents and candy canes. Limit graphic devices to one or two per page, and even then alternate thematic with nonthematic: the Christmas star shining over Bethlehem can alternate with a children's choir (choirs perform at any time of the year); children in pilgrim hats suggestive of Thanksgiving can alternate with representations of nature subjects.

Choose the newsletter's paper color tactfully. Printshops and photocopy stores now stock paper in dozens of different colors, from black to silver to lavender to chartreuse, for a price only a little higher than that of standard white paper. Some newsletter editors take advantage of this abundance by splashing covers with fire engine red to signify Christmas, vivid liturgical purple for Easter, goldenrod-yellow for spring, even a rainbow of colors to suggest "The Many Dimensions of

God's Love." Bright, vivid colors make reading the text a strain, and different colors in the same issue look disorganized. Subdued shades and off tones can increase audience interest considerably, but don't try to overwhelm your audience with colors or color symbolism. Print the cover only or the entire newsletter on a color of paper suggestive of nothing more profound than the season: shades of light green, yellow, and blue for spring; green, amber, and gold for summer; gold, blue, and orange for autumn; and red, green, and silver for winter.

Holiday-Related Themes

During the Middle Ages every other day was a holiday of some sort, an opportunity to celebrate the life of a saint or biblical figure, an event in the life of Christ, or just the passing seasons. Today we have very few holidays left, and those remaining represent little more than a three-day weekend. (When was the last time you really thought about the significance of Labor Day?) Organizing your newsletter around holiday themes can help revive the excitement and enthusiasm previously felt for Labor Day or Pentecost by examining their significance for contemporary Christians.

To get you started, here are fifteen holidays from the Christian and secular calendars that can be used as imaginative, inspiring newsletter themes.

Epiphany (January). The Renaissance Twelfth Night, the Eastern Orthodox Christmas, traditionally the day on which the three wise men brought gifts to the Christ child. Article ideas:

"The Real Christmas" (informational article).
"What Gift Will You Bring to Jesus This Year?" (survey of Sunday school children, teenagers, or adults).

Interview with church member from an Eastern Orthodox background: childhood memories, finding Christ, etc.

"The Gift I Cherish Most" (personal reflection).

Martin Luther King, Jr.'s Birthday (January). A three-day weekend in most states, the birthday of one of the major political leaders of the twentieth century. Article ideas:

"Politics from the Pulpit?" (historical article about the political activism of Christians from the Reformation to the present).

"Has the Dream Been Deferred?" (informational article about race relations in contemporary churches).

Interview with the pastor of an African-American congregation in the community.

"I Have a Dream" (excerpt from Rev. King's speech, with clip-art illustrations).

Valentine's Day (February). Originally a Christian holiday celebrating agapé, or unselfish love; only in the nineteenth century did it turn into an opportunity for high school sweethearts to exchange boxes of candy. Article ideas:

"The Real Valentine's Day" (historical article, but not if you used "The Real Christmas" in January).

"Third Graders in Love" (informational article about decreasing age of the beginning of romantic interest depicted in the secular media).

"Three Kinds of Love" (inspirational article about eros, philos, and agapé).

Interview with the oldest couple in the congregation: childhood memories, meeting, courtship.

Arbor Day (April). Don't laugh. Judaism has an important religious holiday, Tu B'Shevat, dedicated solely to the cultivation and preservation of trees. Article ideas:

"Saving the Earth" (informational article about the Christian's duty to preserve the ecological system).

"A Walk Through the Churchyard" (kinds of plants, flowers, and trees in the church lawn or parking lot).

"Have You Given a Bouquet Today?" (inspirational article; a "bouquet" is any act of kindness).

"The Lily of the Valley" (inspirational article about the plants and flowers used as Christian symbols).

Palm Sunday (usually in April). A theme on Palm Sunday can provide a welcome change of pace from the many magazines that use Easter themes. Article ideas:

"The Entry into Jerusalem" (inspirational article).

"Triumphal Entries" (inspirational article about triumphs that turn into defeats, and then into triumphs again).

"Why Palm Fronds?" (historical article about the use of palm fronds to welcome kings in ancient times).

"What Happened During Easter Week?" (day-by-day analysis using a harmony of the Gospels).

Pentecost (usually in May). Fifty days after Easter, a celebration of the origin of the Christian church. Article ideas:

"The First Day of the Church" (inspirational article).

"The Day Our Church Began" (historical article).

"The Upper Room" (survey: how prayer caused turning points in the lives of members of the congregation).

"Trinity Sunday" (inspirational article).

Cinco de Mayo (May). Mexican Independence Day, celebrated by millions of Mexican-Americans throughout the United States and Canada, and occasionally by others of Hispanic descent. Article ideas:

"What is Cinco de Mayo?" (informational article).

"The Hispanic Church: What is It Doing Right?" (informational article about Hispanic evangelical churches in your community).

Interview with director of your church's Hispanic outreach program or a Mexican-American church member.

"Enseñamos Español" (a vocabulary of general Christian and evangelistic words and phrases in Spanish).

Mother's Day (May). Sometimes overworked, but Mother's Day is practically expected as the theme of the May issue. Article ideas:

"Who's the Mother in Our House?" (reflection from a father raising his children alone).

"What I Remember Most About My Mother" (survey of adults).

Interview with the oldest mother in the congregation.

"How Mother's Day Began" (historical article).

Flag Day (June). No other country reveres its flag as much as does the United States. An effective topic, provided that you don't use other patriotic topics nearby, such as Memorial Day in May or Independence Day in July. Article ideas:

"How We Got Our Flag" (historical article).

"Flags of the World" (informational article).

"The Care and Feeding of Your Flag" (informational article).

"The Christian Flag" (inspirational article).

Father's Day (June). An often neglected holiday, but probably should not follow a May newsletter theme of Mother's Day. Article ideas:

"What's a Father For?" (inspirational article).

"Quality Time" (survey of how fathers in the congregation spend time with their children).

Interview with the oldest father in the congregation.

"How Father's Day Began" (historical article).

Independence Day (July). The only secular holiday in the United States which has not been moved to a Monday; the most important holiday of the summer. Article ideas:

"What Does Independence Mean?" (inspirational article on religious freedom).

Interview with a veteran or veterans in the congregation.

"How We Got Our Flag" (if a similar article hasn't been used for Flag Day in June).

"Independence Days Around the World" (informational article).

Friendship Day (August). Our society is so obsessed with romantic love that it often minimizes the importance of friendship. Article ideas:

"Making and Keeping Friends" (informational article).

"Friendship in the Bible" (informational article).

"Everyday Friends" (inspirational article about daily kindnesses, etc.).

"Your Best Friend" (inspirational article about friendship with God).

Labor Day (September). The only holiday in the calendar dedicated to honoring work. Also marks the unofficial beginning of autumn. Article ideas:

"People of God at Work" (informational article about the occupations of biblical and historical figures).

"Christ in the Marketplace" (inspirational article).

"Everybody Has a Job to Do" (inspirational article).

"What I Want To Do When I Grow Up" (survey of Sunday school children).

Columbus Day (October). Columbus has fallen into disrespect recently, but the values he used to stand for—curiosity, faith, and courage—can still be valid. Article ideas:

"The Faith of Columbus" (inspirational article).

"We're All Explorers" (inspirational article).

Interview with member of the congregation who has recently immigrated to the United States.

"A Nation of Many Faces" (informational article about the ethnic communities in your city).

Thanksgiving Day (November). Thanksgiving is a bit of a problem, because although it is officially dedicated to being thankful, most of us associate the holiday with eating. Fillers for Thanksgiving Day are plentiful; articles come a little harder. Some possibilities:

"How Thanksgiving Became a Holiday" (it didn't start with the pilgrims).

"What I Like Best About Thanksgiving" (survey of Sunday school children).

Interview with member of the congregation who has recently immigrated to the United States and is new to the holiday.

"Thanksgiving All Year Round" (inspirational article).

Advent (December). The four Sundays preceding Christmas. Advent can be a welcome change of pace from Christmas. Use lavender or pink paper. Article ideas:

"Christ is Coming" (inspirational article).

"Making Christmas Christian" (informational article).

"Christmas in July?" (informational article about the probable true birthdate of Jesus).

Interview with an older person in the congregation: "Christmas memories."

Christmas and Easter

These two holidays, the holiest in the Christian year, often represent unbridled aggravation for newsletter staff members. After being overwhelmed by holiday-related commercials and TV programs, songs on the radio, office and school parties, holiday sales in every department store, holiday issues of every popular magazine, they rarely have the drive or the energy to come up with creative article ideas. Any articles they do write are almost sure to bore an audience jaded by big-budget, celebrity-studded network specials. In addition, they are busier than at any other time of the year, weighted down with church, home, school, and office commitments. No wonder Christmas and Easter newsletters are often nothing but front-to-back announcements and fillers.

Contrary to common belief, it is not essential to devote the December and March or April issues of every church newsletter to Christmas and Easter, respectively. It is not unchristian or sacrilegious. After all, most of the event announcements for the month will be for holiday-related programs, parties, and special services anyway, so the newsletter will automatically have a Christmas or Easter "feel." A theme of "Christian Maturity" in December or "Raising Children in the Lord" in April could prove a refreshing change of pace.

If you must organize your themes around Christmas and Easter, try assigning articles six months in advance. Professional magazines do this all the time: a deadline of May or June for Christmas articles and September or October for Easter articles is essential to meet the constraints of publication schedules. It's a bit of a stretch for most writers to think about Christmas in June, but they do have more free time then, and freedom from the barrage of Christmas messages prevalent in December. A few Christmas articles readily available on diskette or in your files will make the December newsletter meetings much less stressful.

You may also choose a more specialized topic than the generic holiday, to give staff writers and volunteers more guidance at a particularly busy and stressful time of the year. Instead of "Christmas," try "The Annunciation," "Advent," "Visitors to the Manger," "Gifts of the Wise

Men," "Christmas Around the World." Instead of Easter, try "Palm Sunday," "Holy Week," "The Last Supper," "Passover and Easter." The possibilities are limitless.

Seasonal, Nonholiday-Related Themes

While "Springtime," "Summer Vacations," "Autumn Joys," and "Winter" come immediately to mind, the best seasonal, nonholiday-related themes celebrate specific, significant days that have not been recognized as official holidays by the government or the Christian church. You can find many interesting possibilities in two essential books: Francis Xavier Weiser's *Handbook of Christian Feasts and Customs: The Year of the Lord in Liturgy and Folklore* (New York: Paulist Press, 1963), which has a Roman Catholic orientation; and Ruth W. Gregory's, *Anniversaries and Holidays* (Chicago: American Library Association, 1983). Check biographical dictionaries and the "This Day in History" page in your local newspaper for other dates that are important to the history of Christianity or Western civilization.

Also, do not discount the history of your own denomination. Phineas F. Brisee founded the Church of the Nazarene in December 1907; a Nazarene newsletter could devote its December issue to "The Story of the Nazarenes." On what date did John Wesley find his heart "strangely warmed" at Aldersgate? When did the Presbyterian Church (U.S.A.) reunite after over a century of separation? When was the first Baptist church in North America founded? When was your local church chartered? When did you move to your present building? A theme commemorating events of importance to your local church or denomination can be as meaningful as a theme devoted to a major Christian holiday.

Timeless Themes

Themes not related to any particular time of the year are referred to as *timeless*. These themes give the newsletter staff a chance to let their imaginations go. Anything relevant to the Bible, God, the Christian life, or the life of the church can be used as a newsletter theme: "Names of God," "The Cross," "Family and Friends," "The Christian Home," "Witnessing," "Revivals," "The Pastoral Life," "Stewardship," "Raising a Christian Child," "Teenagers," "Using Your Talents," "Finding God in Nature," "Growing in Christ," "Singles Today," "Great Christian Writers," "Sunday School," "Christian Hymns," "Getting to Know Your Bible," "Church Attendance," "World Missions," "The Second Coming of Christ," "Finding God at Work," "Our Senior Citizens," "Married and Christian," "Church History," "Deciding What's Right," "The Christian's Working World," and "The Christian's Secret of a Happy Life," are just a few possibilities.

Do not let your imagination go too wild, however. Before you announce a theme to the congregation and solicit articles, ask yourself the following five questions:

Will this theme be interesting to the newsletter's intended audience? Trained theologians may be fascinated by a newsletter theme on "The Uses of the Term *Son of Man* in the Pseudopigrapha," but such a theme will prompt the average church member to flip back to the individual announcements, and the unchurched to throw the newsletter away altogether and check the television schedule. "Raising a Christian Child" will be of interest primarily to individuals who happen to be raising children, "The Single Christian" to those who are single. Of course, you can still use "The Single Christian" if your intended audience is mostly married, but you will have to intersplice thematic articles with exceptionally interesting nonthematic articles and fillers to keep them reading.

Is this theme too similar to one recently used? "Finding God at Work" will generate many of the same sorts of articles as "Labor Day," and "Church History" may veer too close to "Pentecost" for comfort. You may notice that I did not list any themes at all on "God and Country." So many patriotic holidays are in the secular calendar already that nonholiday related patriotic themes are bound to be redundant.

Is this theme overused in general? Regardless of whether your particular newsletter has used them before or not, some themes get so much exposure in professional Christian magazines and the secular media that they stand little chance of success: "The Christian Response to the AIDS Crisis" and "Televangelism," for instance. Other potential themes are vague or simply trite: "Back to School," "The Birth of Spring," "Christian Living."

Is this theme upbeat? Variations of "Finding Christ in Tragedy," "When Death Claims Someone Close to You," and "Victory Over Illness" are the mainstay of many professional religious magazines and they do have a place as articles in the newsletter, but the theme itself should always be positive and uplifting. For the same reason, references to sin, hell, and eternal damnation should occur only tangentially: Convicting sinners is a job for the Holy Spirit and personal evangelism teams, not a newsletter.

Do article ideas come easily to mind? Some themes, such as "Christian Driving" or "Kicking Bad

Habits," sound good on paper, but when it comes time to suggest ideas for interesting, tasteful articles, they are not so good after all. Other potential themes, such as "Christian Celebrities" or "The Soviet Church: Crisis and Transformation," support dozens of possible article ideas, but most of them require more research time and expense than newsletter staff writers have available. If you're going to fly to Hollywood to interview a Christian celebrity, the resulting article belongs in *The Moody Magazine* or *Christianity Today*. There's no point in considering the theme "Diverse Cultures in the Body of Christ" if your church's membership roster does not contain several immigrants from Europe, Latin America, or Asia.

Finding Fillers Fast   7

Two blank pages staring out of your computer screen at two A.M. the morning after your printer's deadline? No problem; just grab one of your books of fillers and leaf through for something of the appropriate length.

Fillers are nothing more than very short articles, usually less than fifty words (although a few are long enough to be considered full-length articles in their own right). What makes them the newsletter editor's best friend, however, is the fact that they've already been researched, written, published, and in most cases cross indexed. All you have to do is input them. In a pinch you can just clip one out of the book and paste it onto a page of camera-ready text, but this method is not recommended: first, it ruins the reference book, and second, the filler text will always look different from the rest of the text on the page, making the newsletter a slipshod montage of type styles and formats.

All Kinds of Fillers

Inspirational and informational. The most popular fillers come in some of the same varieties as ordinary articles. Inspirational and informational fillers and some creative pieces accumulated specifically for church newsletter use can be found in George W. Knight's four volumes of *Church Bulletin Bits* (Grand Rapids, Mich.: Baker Book House, various dates). Another useful reserve of fillers is the short anecdotes used for sermon illustrations. Walter B. Knight's *Master Book of New Illustrations* (Grand Rapids, Mich.: Eerdmans, 1990) and Michael P. Green's *Illustrations for Biblical Preaching* (Grand Rapids, Mich.: Baker Book House, 1988) are probably available in your pastor's library. Eleanor Doan's two-volume *Speaker's Sourcebook* (Grand Rapids, Mich.: Zondervan, 1988 and 1989) is designed for public speakers, but many of her anecdotes, illustrations, and quotations can be modified for church newsletter fillers as well.

For very short (one or two lines) inspirational and informational fillers, you will need one or more books of quotations. *Bartlett's Familiar Quotations*, 13th ed. (Boston: Little, Brown & Company, 1955) has been the standard reference for 150 years, and some of the quotations are no longer all that familiar. It should be supplemented by the more recent *Penguin Dictionary of Quotations* (New York: Penguin Books, 1960), the *Oxford Dictionary of Quotations* (New York: Oxford University Press, 1979), and perhaps something very recent such as *Simpson's Contemporary Quotations: The Most Notable Quotes Since 1950* (Boston: Houghton Mifflin, 1988), the *Penguin Dictionary of Modern Quotations* (New York: Penguin Books, 1988), and the *Penguin Dictionary of Modern Humorous Quotations* (New York: Penguin Books, 1988).

For short poems, the Norton anthologies of British and American literature are worth keeping around the newsletter office, if you or your children happen to have them left over from college, and *The Best Loved Poems of the American People*, edited by Hazel Fellerman (New

York: Doubleday, 1936) is essential. Otherwise pick up *The Oxford Book of American Verse*, edited by F. O. Matthiessen (New York: Oxford University Press, 1990), or *The Oxford Book of American Light Verse*, edited by William Harmon (New York: Oxford University Press, 1979).

For short humorous prose, try *American Humor*, edited by Arthur P. Dudden (New York: Oxford University Press, 1987), Frank Muir's *Oxford Book of Humorous Prose* (New York: Oxford University Press, 1990), and the various joke books by Tal D. Bonham (*Treasury of Clean Church Jokes, Treasury of Clean Jokes for Children, Treasury of Clean Teenage Jokes, Treasury of Clean Sports Jokes*, and others) published by Broadman Press (Nashville: various dates). Be careful, however, because unlike quotations and anecdotes designed specifically for reproduction, poems, humorous prose, and jokes may be copyrighted. Check the title page of the book in question, or limit your choices to anonymous authors and authors who died before 1930.

Household hints are popular with both male and female readers in secular magazines and newsletters. We all are interested in the best way to get grass stains off jeans or to repair a leaky faucet. This sort of filler should be used sparingly, however, in a church newsletter designed to draw people's minds away from everyday tasks like household maintenance. No one wants to read about God's plan for salvation on the same page as how to make furniture polish out of mayonnaise. If you're desperate to try something different, and they are around the house anyway, you might consider adapting (not copying) a section from *How to Do Just About Anything* (New York: Reader's Digest Books, 1986), *The Good Housekeeping Illustrated Book of Home Maintenance*

(New York: Hearst Books, 1985), or *Hints! from Heloise* (New York: Avon, 1981). But don't rush out to buy them with money from the newsletter budget.

Recipes have the same popularity as household hints, and the same drawback: A meditation about the cross could conceivably end up on the same page with Sister Martha's baked squash surprise. However, if recipes are donated by members of the congregation instead of dug out of a cookbook, they could fill the same function as creative pieces. Someone who would never dream of picking up a pencil or booting up a computer can still be made to feel like a valuable part of the newsletter team by donating a favorite recipe for three-bean salad or marshmallow pie. Create a file of recipe fillers by asking around at potlucks and other church gatherings, with the understanding that the recipes donated may or may not be printed at an unspecified later date. Then, when you need a filler for the individual announcements page of the August issue, by all means pull out the baked squash surprise. Make sure that all recipes printed are seasonal: no barbecued chicken and corn on the cob in December, no ginger-bread men in June.

Cartoons in either single-panel or three-panel formats always interest readers. Many of us look forward to turning to the comics page of the newspaper first to check on the exploits of Garfield before finding out what's happening in the Middle East, and the same principle can be applied to the newsletter. While too many cartoons are difficult to incorporate and can make the newsletter look like the Sunday *Times-Herald* comics page, one or two per issue can add variety and visual appeal. Church-related cartoons in public domain are available in the two volumes of Phil Jackson's

Ready-to-Use Cartoons for Church Publications (Grand Rapids, Mich.: Baker, various dates), Howard Paris's *Clip-Art Panel Cartoons for Churches* (Grand Rapids, Mich.: Baker, 1984), and six volumes of George W. Knight's *Instant Cartoons for Church Newsletters* (Grand Rapids, Mich.: Baker, various dates).

The only problem with cartoons is that they have to be clipped out and pasted on, which is a little tricky for beginners. After some practice, however, incorporating a single-panel or three-panel cartoon into your newsletter should take only a few minutes, and it will be well worth the effort.

Talented artists in the congregation will often volunteer single-panel black-and-white cartoons. As long as the images are dark and not overly detailed, most photocopying machines can shrink the cartoons down to one- or two-inch squares for cutting and pasting.

Do not, however, suggest that your talented artist draw a cartoon of Snoopy ushering children into Sunday school or Bart Simpson officiating at choir practice. Using trademarked characters may seem cute, but it leaves you open for a mammoth lawsuit. Even if cartoonists agree that going to Sunday school or singing in the choir is a good idea, they must still keep close tabs on their creations to avoid having them slip into public domain: then images of Bart Simpson or Snoopy could promote taverns and adult book stores, with no legal recourse possible for their creators.

Quizzes, games, and **puzzles**, the standby of children's magazines, can be pleasant diversions in newsletters intended for all ages, as long as they are not overly simple and do not appear in every issue. Quizzes ("How Much Do You Know about the Patriarchs?"; "How Much Do You Know about the Apostles?"; "Name that Parable") work best, since they require few special graphics (most word processing packages will not print the answers upside down, so you may have to print them out on a separate sheet of paper, then cut and paste). Games and puzzles, including crossword puzzles, anagrams, and word scrambles, require graphics that are probably not available in your word processing program or are too time consuming to be practical. They will have to be cut and pasted like cartoons. For ready-made quizzes, games, and puzzles, get the two volumes of Frank R. Reynolds's *Bible Quizzes for Church Newsletters* (Grand Rapids, Mich.: Baker Book House, various dates), Erma Reynolds's *Bible People Quiz Book* (Grand Rapids, Mich.: Baker Book House, 1979), and the *Bible Quiz Book* (New York: Morehouse Publications, 1979). To make up your own quizzes and puzzles, the *All the . . .* series by Herbert Lockyer (Grand Rapids, Mich.: Zondervan Publishing Corporation, 1988) is invaluable. From it you can find out about every apostle mentioned in the Bible; every book and chapter; biblical doctrine; man, woman, and child; king and queen; holy day and holiday; parable, prayer, and promise; trade and occupation; and messianic prophecy. The series has fourteen volumes so far, and no sign of losing momentum.

Clip-art consists of stylized borders, church buildings, balloons, birds, trumpets, members of the congregation going about various church activities, various likenesses of Jesus and the apostles: simple pieces of art that, when used judiciously, can enliven monotonous pages of text. Like cartoons, clip-art usually must be cut out of a book and pasted onto your text. A number of computer companies are now offering clip-art on diskette (see appendix for suggestions), but if you're not ready for the sometimes-tricky software maneuvering necessary to pull up clip-art on screen, try

George W. Knight's *Clip-Art Features for Church Newsletters,* in six volumes (Grand Rapids, Mich.: Baker Book House, various dates) and Steve Hunt and Dave Adamson's *Church Clip-Art Book* (Grand Rapids, Mich.: Zondervan Publishing Corporation, 1988). Tom Finley has put together hundreds of borders, edges, captions, and other graphics in his *Church Bulletin Clip Art Book* (Ventura, Calif.: Gospel Light Publications, 1986), *Church Ministry Clip Art Book* (Ventura, Calif.: Gospel Light Publications, 1988), and clip-art books designed for children and teens. Chuck McMurray's two-volume *Cathedral Clip-Art for Churches* (Long Prairie, Minn.: Cathedral Press, Inc., 1986) is oversized and rather unwieldy, but comprehensive in scope.

Photographs fill the same needs for variety and visual appeal as cartoons or clip-art, but since they illustrate one of the newsletter's major announcements or news stories, they have an immediacy lacking in other nontext graphics. (There is little room in newsletters for "art photos" of people or places not used to illustrate an article.) When interviewing the new director of personal evangelism, why not include a photograph of him, either borrowed from his private files or taken specifically for the purpose? Good wallet-sized photographs can be printed or photocopied without damage; other sizes must be cut down, or cropped, to fit the confines of the newsletter format. The single-person portrait, the most popular subject of all photographers, becomes nearly the only useful subject for newsletter photographs; crowds, mountains, and deserted seashores lose considerable interest when shrunk down into a one- or two-inch square. Even groups, five members of a Sunday school class or the pastor and his wife, are risky. Stick to a single person, sitting, standing, or walking, usually shot from the waist up.

To be reproduced well, the photograph should have a glossy finish, not matting or a silver finish. Black-and-white works best, though professional printshops can do wonders with halftones. It's a good idea to keep negatives of all photos to be reproduced, just in case.

Like other types of fillers, photographs should be used sparingly and put in locations on the page that will catch the reader's eye: usually the bottom or center right. An additional stipulation, however, is that photographs should always be placed near the articles they illustrate, usually above or below, sometimes to the right or left.

Using Fillers

With such a wealth of resources available, it is no wonder that some newsletters are composed of nothing but events announcements and fillers, thrown together with no apparent organization or emphasis. The most effective newsletter staff members, however, choose newsletter fillers with the same careful thought that they use in choosing more substantial articles.

Choose fillers in advance. Some editors don't worry about fillers at all, then seem surprised when they have input everything and there's room left. The truth is that no number of full-sized articles will fit perfectly into your four- or eight-page newsletter, and even if they could, the resulting pages would look bland and monotonous, like a business report. You will need at least one filler per page for every issue, so why not leaf through your reference books in advance, choosing eight or nine possibilities?

Keep the intended audience in mind. "Ten Reasons Why We Should Win Sinners" will not go over very well in an evangelistic newsletter, since no one likes to think that he's a sinner being won. "A Godly Father" may depress rather than inspire those whose fathers were less than godly. Treat the filler not as superfluous—just a way to avoid blank space—but as an integral part of the newsletter, and make your selections based on the needs of the newsletter's intended audience.

Keep the theme in mind. Fillers should be chosen because they relate to the newsletter's theme ("Thomas Jefferson's Prayer" for the Independence Day issue, "A Mother's Beatitudes" for the Mother's Day issue), or because they relate to the major articles on the page ("Kids Can Be Christians, Too" on a page devoted primarily to children's news, "The Church Needs More Workers" on a page devoted primarily to individual announcements and opportunities to serve). Alternately, if there are already many articles related to the theme, a completely different filler may provide welcome variety: a one-panel cartoon on tithing for the Christmas issue, "Tips for Christian Students" in the Easter issue, a recipe for blueberry pie in an issue devoted to "The Church in the World." Make sure, of course, that the filler doesn't conflict with the theme: no Christmas fillers in July, and the recipe for blueberry pie *does not* belong in an issue devoted to "The Challenge of World Hunger."

Use fillers sparingly. While they perform an important function in breaking up the page and capturing audience interest, fillers can be overused, giving the newsletter an unappealing, choppy look and a superficial feel. Limit your fillers to three per page.

Vary the types of fillers. A newsletter full of tearjerking anecdotes on "Mother's Hands of Love" will send the most sentimental reader into insulin shock, and "Daffynitions" separating each article will leave readers wondering whether you're printing a newsletter or Joan Rivers' latest standup comedy routine. If there's room for five fillers, use five different types of fillers: an inspirational anecdote, an informational filler about the use of bread in the Bible (or something similar), a humorous quotation, a piece of clip-art, and a recipe or household hint.

Keep careful records of fillers used. "I thought we decided *against* that filler last time" is no excuse for printing the same filler in two consecutive newsletters, or even in newsletters published months apart. No filler, not even an exceptional one, should be reprinted for at least two years. To avoid this problem, some newsletter editors go through their reference books and cross out fillers as they use them. Others prefer to keep their books undamaged and use a more complex system of recording the name and date of each filler used, its reference source, and page number, and then double check before each new use (an easy feat if your record file is on the computer, tedious if it's in a notebook).

Edit fillers to make them sound local. Since the fillers have to be retyped anyway, there is no reason why exotic locations cannot be transformed into somewhere close to home. A man walking through Hyde Park in London or New York's Central Park can easily be walking down Main Street in your town. Any church mentioned could become the Bethany Assembly of God; an unidentified shopping area could become Park Forest Mall. Do not use the names of real people, however, even with their permission; this can result in all sorts of problems months or years down the line.

Update old-fashioned fillers. Many valuable anecdotes and quotations were written generations ago and contain references that sound odd or even incomprehensible today: coal tar, castor oil, buggies, blacksmiths, green grocers, streetcars. Update these references to gasoline, Alka-Seltzer, Toyotas, auto mechanics, 7-11 clerks, and R-buses (or the local equivalent). A warning about the evils of magic lantern shows can easily be updated to a warning about the latest Hollywood thriller at the Cineplex.

One filler book contains a poem about a child's plastic years. *Plastic* used to mean pliable or impressionable, so the poem is really about the years in which a child can be molded to walk in the ways of the Lord. Nowadays, however, *plastic* has a completely different connotation: synthetic, superficial, false, as in phrases like "our plastic society." To avoid unplanned chuckling in the congregation, any newsletter editor who desperately loves that poem will have to change *plastic* to *pliable* and not worry about the meter.

All about Editing 8

It's June 12, warm, and still rather bright even though the sun has gone down. The choir can be heard practicing "To Be Used of God" far off in the sanctuary. On the desk before you are three articles on the July theme "God Speaks Through Nature," two typed on a Smith-Corona, one scrawled on a legal pad. Two of the articles are indescribably bad. You also have three local and two national news articles, three events announcements, two individual announcements, the "Pastor's Podium" on official church stationery, a photo and profile of the new youth minister, and ten good fillers. The rest of the newsletter staff is out at the Pizza Hut, congratulating themselves over extra cheese and pepperoni and pitchers of soda. It's up to you, the editor, to congeal this mass of words into a well-organized, interesting, effective newsletter. What now? The transformation of text into a well-organized, effective newsletter involves careful planning, sensitivity to the visual appeal of a text page, and a good computer.

Article Selection and Inputting

First, read through every submission and determine what *must* be printed. Mass-market publications commonly receive two or three hundred submissions for each one they use; the church newsletter will not receive nearly that number. Unfortunately, being a nonprofit, volunteer publication eager for volunteer submissions, the church newsletter is obligated to print virtually everything it receives. Articles received from church members who aren't on the staff are *always* printed, with two exceptions: Some articles may be rejected for lack of space (this is usually a good policy to use to omit rambling opinion pieces), and others may be rejected because they are not edifying to the community (not religious in content, deviate from church doctrine, libelous, etc.). Every other inspirational article, informational article, or creative piece a church member goes out of his or her way to write gets included, albeit sometimes in an abridged and heavily edited version. Of course, it is perfectly all right to *hold* a submission, as long as you contact the writer and tactfully explain why publication must be postponed.

Articles assigned to staff members are never postponed or rejected, but are printed in the issue for which they were assigned. Nonassigned articles from staff members may be either postponed for lack of space or rejected outright. Staff writers, used to producing many articles, should not be easily offended by rejection.

Events announcements are always printed. Individual announcements may sometimes be rejected, but only in exceptional circumstances: for instance, if Sister Flegelbaum feels compelled to inform everyone that her grandson, who lives in Amarillo and has never even visited the church, made the honor roll at Prairie Plains State College. If her grandson *did* attend your church, the announcement would make it into the newsletter, of course, but announcements about people beyond the local congregation are normally not included. Also, if Sister Flegelbaum decided to make her announcement for three issues in a row, the newsletter editor would be well within rights to reject it.

Next, read through the articles again, and determine what *should* be printed. Which news stories or inspirational / informational articles are most relevant to the theme? Which would be the most meaningful to the newsletter's primary audience? Which are most interesting in their own right? Omit stories of minor interest and those that seem too close to stories printed in the last few issues; "Church Attendance on the Rise in the United States" in June virtually precludes printing "Revival of Religious Devotion in the United States" in August.

Input each article into a separate computer file. Computer-literate staff writers (and after a few issues, all staff writers will become computer-literate) submit their articles in both hard copies (that is, on paper) and on diskettes; so theoretically the newsletter editor just has to boot up the computer, shove the disk in drive A, and key "Retrieve." In the real world, however, many articles will be submitted in hard copy format only, and those on diskette may have been produced on different computers at home, at school, at the office, or even at the photocopy store. Macintosh and IBM computer files can be incompatible; different software packages for the same computer system, even marginally different versions of the same software package, may be incompatible. (Have you ever tried accessing a document in Word-Perfect 5.1 from WordPerfect 5.0?) File conversion programs will convert documents between various software types, and even between the Macintosh and IBM operating systems, but a conversion may delete essential formatting: fonts, point sizes, clip-art, columns, tables, headers and footers. Articles not created with the same word processing program the newsletter editor uses will require formatting, either by the editor or by a staff assistant. It's not as tedious as it sounds. Formatting with a word processor is not time-consuming. Considerable time can be saved by converting as much data as your system will allow.

Editing

Make corrections. Many fledgling newsletter editors perceive their jobs as little more than correcting typos, changing "Its time for a revival" to "It's time for a revival" and "there Bibles" to "their Bibles." Correcting the grammar, punctuation, and spelling in the text *is* important, mainly because these are the problems most likely to bother readers. Software packages are available to check spelling and some grammatical errors, but their level of accuracy is open to dispute, and many are more trouble than they are worth. Unless you are a longtime freshman composition teacher and have every rule of grammar internalized, keep dictionaries, grammar handbooks, and other reference books nearby during editing (see appendix for suggested titles).

Check facts. More important than copy editing, though often unnoticed by the readers, is to correct the writers' research. Make sure that all of the necessary facts are present in each article. *When* does the installation service begin? *Whom* should we contact for tickets to the bake-off? *What* is the name of Bob and Gloria Brubacker's new baby? Also make sure that the facts presented are accurate. Is the Sunday school superintendent's old phone number listed instead of his new one? Was the church founded in 1911 or 1917? Was Martin Luther born in Bavaria or Thuringia? Professional fact checking, which involves tracking down every name, date, place, and quotation, is probably not necessary for a church newsletter. A good guideline is to check only when the fact involves a member of the congregation, or when you have a reasonable doubt in your mind: Is it *Jeffery* or *Jeffrey* Dennis?

Do the fact checking over a period of several days, to give you time to call the chair of the Easter sunrise service committee to determine if we *really* need to be there by 5:00 A.M. before putting that information in print.

Cut libelous, bigoted, damaging, or un-Christlike statements that haven't already been weeded out: "Catholics and other pagans . . ."; "Our mayor is like the Antichrist in that . . ."; "The Christian Prayer League is full of backbiters. . . ." Newsletter articles are no place for polemic or disputes; make sure that any visitor or unchurched neighbor who happens to walk into the sanctuary and picks up the newsletter will find nothing but articles about the body of Christ.

Edit for concise, vigorous, specific, and stylistically appropriate writing. The newsletter editor should try to transform the text of each article into competent (if not brilliant) English prose. Study Strunk and White's *Elements of Style*, Rudolph Flesch's *The Art of Readable Writing*, and William Zinsser's *On Writing Well* (see appendix for details), and while you're at it, keep these brief rules of style posted in plain sight of your computer:

1. *Cut every unnecessary word*, even if you like it a lot.
   "*Basically,* our church is *undergoing* change" to
   "Our church is changing."
   "*There are* many decisions *to be made* by *the members of* this congregation *in regard* to the building program" to

"This congregation must make many decisions regarding the building program.

"The new choir robes will be blue *in color*" to
"The new choir robes will be blue."

2. *Change passive verbs to active verbs* whenever possible.
"Rev. Termite *was honored* by the Minor Prophets Club" to
"The Minor Prophets Club honored Rev. Termite."

The sermon *was preached* by Dr. Louis Goforit, professor emeritus of theology at Wetrainem Seminary" to
"Dr. Louis Goforit, professor emeritus of theology at Wetrainem Seminary, preached the sermon."

"It *was usual* for us to pray before dinner" to
"We usually prayed before dinner."

3. *Change vague words to specific words.* You may have to increase the word count considerably.
"Rev. Termite has a *variety of outside interests*" to
"Rev. Termite collects pre-Columbian feathered headdresses from Guatemala and enjoys tennis, horseback riding, and mountain climbing." These new words are not considered unnecessary, since they add interesting information.

"It was a *nice day* for a picnic" to
"It was a warm, clear day, with a few scattered clouds and a bright sun: perfect for the Little Shepherds League picnic."

"Today's children face *many problems*" to "Today's children face drugs, alcohol, and many other problems."

4. *Modify language that is too colloquial or too formal.* "Mrs. Hughes' senior high class had an awesome time at a mondo mega-party last Saturday night" to "Mrs. Hughes' senior high class threw a great party last Saturday night."

"It behooves each of us to invest some time in contemplating our individual destiny in the eschaton" to "Where are you going to spend eternity?"

"The rescue mission extends its thanks to the food drive team for its magnanimity" to "The rescue mission thanks the food drive for its hard work and generosity."

5. *Don't waste much time agonizing over minor examples of wordiness, passives, vagueness, or faulty style.* "We live in an era of constant change" is fine. Improvable, but fine.

"Then the choir was asked to perform at the Morning Hills Nursing Home" *could* become "Then the choir performed. . . ." But it doesn't have to.

"Our church faces some important decisions." Okay, *decisions* is a little too vague, but if it would take half an hour to track down the author of the article to find out what those decisions are, let the sentence stand.

"At this juncture, the church board recommends hiring a new assistant pastor." *Juncture* could easily be replaced by several less stuffy words, but if you're facing a deadline and you have a choice of thumbing through the thesaurus or tossing a football to your son for the first time all week, *juncture* should stay *juncture*. There's no point in getting ulcers over stylistics. God's work is supposed to be a joy, not an overwhelming burden.

Of course, editing is an ongoing process. You may edit each article two or three times before it sounds right. The rule: Spend time editing the document in proportion to the document's permanence. We all know that Hemingway edited the ending of *The Sun Also Rises* over thirty times, and Tolstoy rewrote every word of his monumental *War and Peace* eight times, but they were hoping to be on the curricula of college English classes and on the alternate selection list of the Book-of-the-Month Club for the next three hundred years. An office memo, to be glanced at once and then tossed into the recycling bin, deserves no more than a single editorial going over. Most newsletter articles will last about a month, so read through them twice, three times at most, and then go on.

Volunteers and, less frequently, staff writers have been known to voice loud objections to any change of the wording of their pet project, sometimes understandably. After working hours or days on a project, it's hard to watch an editor (arbitrarily?) delete a well-turned phrase or carefully thought-out description. Professional writers are used to editors taking liberties with their manuscripts; volunteers are not. Keep copies of the drafts of all volunteer submissions, and be able to justify all changes of more than a few words in an exceptionally gracious manner: "We felt that changing these few words would make your ideas shine through better."

As a last step before layout, add headlines, bylines, and captions. All articles except fillers need short headline descriptions: "Pastor Visits Yugoslavia"; "April Bible Study on Exodus"; "Teen Talent Time." Headlines should be set off from the text of the articles by being larger, in boldface, underlined, or all three. Any format is fine as long as it is consistent. Leave one blank line between the headline and the text, two between the text and the headline of the next article.

Bylines, the word *by* followed by the name of the author of the article, go between the headline and the text. They are usually printed in a size smaller than the text, italicized, or both. Fillers, events announcements, and individual announcements do not require bylines. Some editors omit the bylines of members of the newsletter staff, but unless there are *severe* space restrictions, anyone who takes the trouble to research and write an article deserves a byline.

Captions are simply short descriptions, "headlines" of photographs. They are placed directly beneath the photographs, and like bylines are usually set off from the rest of the text by being smaller, italicized, or both.

Layout

Layout used to be quite a chore, involving endless hours of piecing paragraphs of text together like a jigsaw puzzle, requiring blue pencils, styluses, glue sticks, tape, bottles of glue, straight edges, and a raised drafting table. Today's computer software will allow you to do all of the layout for an eight-page newsletter in an hour or less.

Determine the typeface and style of the newsletter page. This will take some time, but you will probably make a template to use with each issue, so the hardest work will come at the beginning. Newsletter pages are usually divided into two columns, with 35 to 50 characters per column line. Page numbers are not necessary for a four-page newsletter, but an eight-page newsletter should have them at the outside of each page (alternating right-left corner).

The font and point sizes you will use for the text should be determined in advance. *Font* refers to the specific typeface of the text: Times, Helvetica, New Century Schoolbook, and Courier are the most common, but both IBM PCs and Macintoshes offer dozens of choices. Pick a font you like and use it for everything—headlines, bylines, captions, and text; two different fonts may work for special emphasis, but three or more will throw your newsletter into chaos. You may, of course, use a different font for the church logo on the front cover or contact information on the back cover.

Point means the size of the letters in your text. There are 72 points in an inch. Modern word processing programs let you choose any point size you want, even halfsizes, from 6 point (too small to read without a magnifying glass) to 300 point (letters over four inches high). For practical purposes, choose three different point sizes: one for regular text (10 point is the usual), one for bylines and captions (smaller, maybe 8 point), and one for headlines (larger, 12 or 14 point). The newsletter name, church name, or church logo may be printed in a very large size (50 point or more). Otherwise, exercise restraint. A dozen different point sizes will work as well as a dozen different fonts to transform your newsletter into a slipshod mess.

Boldface, underlining, italics, bold italics, shadows, and other special type styles are available for special effects in almost all fonts and point sizes. Use them sparingly.

Word processing programs will do most of the rest of the work for you automatically. Follow the instructions for your specific program to create a template of blank pages, with unchanging text already incorporated. These will resemble the charts in chapter 1, except that they will be full sized and mostly blank, waiting for you to call up articles from the diskette where you input them. Now the fun part begins.

Determine the approximate location of each article in the newsletter, based on the primary audience and theme. Which articles should go on the front cover? Which will take up the back cover? Strive for a variety of article sizes and types (don't cram everything on Christmas together into four pages and then have nothing left), as well as unity (the sorts of articles that naturally belong together). Don't forget that nonchanging information on the front and back covers (logo, times of services, the church's address and telephone number, the names of the pastoral staff members, the names of the newsletter staff members, the church's statement of purpose, a blank half-page for the mailing label and postage) will cut down on the amount of original material to be included on those pages.

Move each article into its proper position on the template (the blank newsletter pages). You will have to modify or move articles so that they fit on the page properly. Make sure that each page looks unified and well organized:

No obtrusive lines or texts.

Neither too much nor too little white space.

No articles beginning at the end of one column and carried over to the top of the next, unless they are an entire page long.

No articles longer than a page, unless they are two
entire pages long.

A mixture of long and short articles, articles of various types, and thematic and nonthematic articles.
But no odd or abrupt juxtapositions of different
types of articles.

No "clumps" of several fillers together. No pages without a filler or another sort of break in the text (photograph, cartoon, clip-art).

You may have to re-edit articles or switch articles
between different pages to make sure every page works
out properly. Be sure to leave room for photos, cartoons, and clip-art.

**Switch, modify, and edit articles until each page is
visually appealing, well organized, and easy to read.**
The sample newsletter page reprinted on the next page
is a mess: three (actually four) events announcements,
one individual announcement, a news story, half of an
inspirational article, and two fillers, all jumbled together
like a soup. See if you can find all of the problems.

The article titled "Western Round-Up" extends from
the bottom of one column to the top of the next; "Easter
in the Soviet Union" begins on one page and ends who
knows where; and there is too much blank space over-
all. The page displays no unity: articles do not have to
be linked thematically, but they should demonstrate a
visual symmetry. The headings are not consistent: sometimes underlined, sometimes boldface, sometimes
absent. You also may have noticed that "Special Note
for Children!" is actually two events announcements
and an individual announcement crammed together
(and the individual announcement really has nothing
to do with children). Important information is left out
of almost every article.

The Ladies' Christian League of the First United Christian Church will meet as always on the second Monday of the month, April 8th, at 7:30 p.m. in the Fellowship Hall. We will be doing a study for April and May led by Donna Kiderowski on "Gifts of the Holy Ghost." Come and join us in our explorations.

***

Special Note for Children!
On Saturday, April 13th, the Young Pioneers will be visiting the San Diego Zoo! Be sure to see Bob Wiley or Rev. Parsnip for details. Also, don't forget the special Junior High Bash in the Fellowship Hall on Saturday, April 20th.

Remember, we are still collecting your California redemptive cans and plastic bottles every Sunday.

***

Tact is the ability to close your mouth before someone else wants to.

Western Round-Up
Put on your ten-gallon hat, grab your cowboy boots, and join us on Saturday, April 27th for a rip-roaring good time!
*Chili
*Bake-off
*Potluck

John and Irma Jackson, who originally hail from Wyoming, will be teaching us some authentic cowboy songs.
Y'all Come!

***

Six Little Ways to Mean More to Your Church
1. Be an On-Timer.
2. Be a Friendly Greeter.
3. Be a Cheerful Giver.
4. Be a Willing Helper.
5. Be a Hymn Singer.
6. Be an Earnest Pray-er.

***

Arnold Talinger
Arnold Talinger, the renowned writer and theologian, visited the United Presbyterian Theological Seminary in our town on March 18th. Rev. Talinger spoke of his years of ministering to children with severe mental and physical handicaps.

***

Easter in the Soviet Union
Tatyana Selenov, the grandmother of Debbie Bates, remembers what Easter was like when she was a little girl living on a farm outside of Moscow. "We had to get up very early to milk the cows, Easter or not," the white-haired octogenerian said. "But sometimes when my sister and I got out to the barn we found

The severely edited version appears on page 111.

Since most of the articles in the previous version were aimed at children and teenagers, the page was revised into a sort of "youth round-up." Consequently, the article on the Ladies' Christian League and the beginning of "Christmas in the Soviet Union" were moved elsewhere. One filler was exchanged with a more youth-oriented quotation, and the other was given a title more appealing to young people: from "Six Little Ways to Mean More to Your Church" to "Making the Most of Your Church" (*little* doesn't go over well with people under twenty-one, and they rarely use the verb *to mean* in this context). Essential information was added to nearly every article. The headlines were made consistent. The lines of stars between articles were deleted, except in the case of the bottom left filler, which was too short to need a headline. The articles in both columns were placed to avoid parallel white spaces.

Make sure that facing page layouts are unified and symmetrical. When people open the newsletter, they will subconsciously regard pages 2 and 3, 4 and 5, and 6 and 7 as units. You don't want long articles to fill both of these page units, or photographs to be placed in clashing locations (center right of one page, top left of the other).

Print out the newsletter text on good bond paper. These four or eight sheets of paper, called camera-ready copy, will be used by the printer or photocopier operator to actually create the newsletter copies. Check that the pages look the way they are supposed to: no text carried over to the next page; articles unified and symmetrical; boldface, underlining, and different point sizes in the right locations; no smudges, black marks, or other imperfections. While this is no time to add or delete substantial blocks of text, you may want to read

ZOO NEWS

On Saturday, April 13th, the Young Pioneers will host an all-day bus trip to the San Diego Zoo. Bob Wiley and Rev. Parsnip will chaperon the trip, which is open to any child between the ages of nine and fifteen. Parents' permission slips are available in the church office.

We will meet in the church parking lot at 8:30 a.m. and return by 6:00 p.m. Children are asked to bring $10.00 to help pay for admission to the zoo and a box lunch. Contact Bob Wiley or the church secretary for more information.

JUNIOR HIGH BASH

All boys and girls in the junior high Sunday school class and their friends are invited to the fellowship hall on Saturday, April 13th, from 8:00 p.m. to midnight. Pizza, soft drinks, and other snacks will be served; party games, music, and the gymnasium facilities will be available, according to the chaperons, Rev. and Mrs. Feldspar.

This will be a lockout party: anybody leaving after 10:00 p.m. stays out. So come early!

****

To do the right thing is the only investment that never fails.

BLESSINGS FROM CHILDREN

Arnold Talinger, the renowned writer and theologian, visited the United Presbyterian Theological Seminary in our town on March 18th. Speaking of his years of ministering to children with severe mental and physical handicaps, Rev. Talinger said, "The blessings I have received from these children are beyond price."

MAKE THE MOST OF YOUR CHURCH

1. Be an on-timer.
2. Be a friendly greeter.
3. Be a cheerful giver.
4. Be a willing helper.
5. Be a hymn singer.
6. Be an earnest pray-er.

WESTERN ROUND-UP

Put on your ten-gallon hat, grab your cowboy boots, and join us on Saturday, April 27th from 10:00 a.m. to 3:00 p.m. in the church parking lot for a rip-roaring good time!

There will be a chili cook-off, a potluck dinner, western costumes, and door prizes. John and Irma Jackson, who originally hail from Wyoming, will teach us some authentic cowboy songs. Contact John Jackson to sign up for the chili cook-off or the potluck.
Y'all come!

through one last time to catch any grammatical errors that slid past during the editing phase. You can always mark errors, correct them, and print out a new page.

If no photographs, cartoons, or clip-art are to be added to the text, the complete newsletter may be printed immediately. For short runs of 200 or fewer copies, laser printers may be used. Simply print out all of the copies of the front and back covers, flip them over, and return them to the paper tray for printing out pages 2 and 3 (2 and 7 of an eight-page newsletter). Do the same for inserts, if any. Using the laser printer for large print runs, however, taxes the time and energy of the most dedicated newsletter staff.

If your computer is not attached to a laser printer, save the newsletter text on a diskette, then take the diskette and your software package somewhere else to do the printing. In this case, of course, you will print out only a single copy and photocopy the rest:

> Photocopy stores and computer stores will print out a copy of word processing files on laser printers for a reasonable price
>
> College and university computer labs often allow students access to laser printers for a nominal fee. Sometimes the laser printers are not in the best condition, however.
>
> Many businesses do not mind if their employees run off a few pages on company-owned laser printers for personal use. Ask your supervisor's permission in advance (unless you are the supervisor), and arrange your schedule so that the printing occurs before or after work hours, or during lunch.

Cut and paste cartoons, puzzles, clip-art, and photographs. Decide what cartoons, puzzles, and clip-art (usually referred to as simply art) you want to use in advance, and make several good photocopies on bond paper. Cut the art from the paper with ordinary scissors, being careful not to leave any ragged edges. Crop all photographs (that is, carefully cut them to the proper size) at the same time. Coat the back of each piece of art with a thin, even layer of glue or paste (glue sticks are available in most office supply stores). Do not use tape. Then carefully affix it to the space you reserved on the newsletter page. Leave at least one quarter-inch of blank space between the art and any blocks of text, and the same margins that you use for the rest of the newsletter. If the art comes out smeared, spindled, or crooked, or overlaps the margins, you will have to print out a new page and start over. If the art overlaps a block of text for any reason, you will have to rework the page, print out a new copy, and start over. The work is not as delicate as it sounds, but it does require concentration. Be sure that kids, dogs, MTV, church janitors, and people who might suddenly prod your shoulder are well out of the way before you begin.

Be sure to save rough drafts and edited versions of each article, as well as copies of the completed newsletter pages on diskettes stored in several places. You don't want any unpleasant surprises later.

Now you are ready to bring the completed camera-ready copy to the printshop or photocopy store.

Be Kind to Your Printer

9

Most church newsletter print runs do not require a printshop. If you plan on only up to 200 copies of the newsletter, on letter- or legal-sized paper, with no color art or photographs, Photocopies-Are-Us or the local equivalent can do the job cheaply and efficiently, and the finished newsletter will not be noticeably different in quality from a newsletter typeset and printed at Park Avenue Printers. Doing the photocopying yourself instead of paying a clerk usually saves two or three cents per copy; go at a nonbusy time to avoid long lines and aggravation. You can also save money by doing your own collating, folding, and stapling, either at the photocopy store or back at the newsletter office.

If you balk at the idea of photocopying the entire newsletter text, consider having the front and back covers printed professionally. In eight-page newsletters, the front and back covers are usually restricted to permanent, unchanging information, so there's no reason why they couldn't include special fonts, point sizes, even specially appointed graphics. Pages 2 and 7, which change every month, would have to be photocopied onto the other side.

For color art or photographs, oversized pages, or print runs of more than 200 copies, the services of a professional printer will keep a few tempers beneath the boiling point. Sometimes members of the congregation own printshops, run the publications department of the local community college, head the editorial department of a local publishing house, teach journalism at a high school, or otherwise have access to free use of an offset printer (and the know-how to run it). If not, you will have to count on expending between 50 and 70 percent of the newsletter budget on printing. There are ways, however, to decrease the printing costs, such as the following.

Ask around town for a printshop owned by a Christian. Who publishes your denominational magazines? Who does the printing for the newsletter of the church down the block? Sometimes Christians give discounts for church newsletters, or even print them for free.

Even other printshops sometimes give discounts to nonprofit organizations and others whose goals they find agreeable. Meet with the owner or manager of the printshop, explain the outreach of your church and the role the newsletter plays, and see what develops.

Printshops in large urban areas often have inflated prices to accommodate higher demand or city and state sales tax. Federal Express, U.P.S., and electronic mail permit newsletter editors to investigate options nationwide and take advantage of sizeable discounts offered by printshops in the less-populated regions of the country.

Be sure to deliver camera-ready copy. Printshops are perfectly willing to accept your newsletter on a diskette, to be accessed, typeset, and printed; a few will accept typewritten copy that has to be input before being typeset and printed. Of course, these services cost extra. Submit newsletter text copy that looks exactly like the finished newsletter pages are supposed to look.

Bring your own paper. Some printers do not allow customers to furnish their own paper, but if they do, a stop by the office supplies store on the way to the printshop can save a few dollars.

Do not ask for miracles. A three-color sunburst rising over an empty tomb would make a stunning front cover for the Easter issue, and most printshops have the equipment to produce it—but not overnight, and not for the same price charged to print out 200 copies of a black-and-white newsletter.

Forget about last-minute changes. After the newsletter text goes to the printshop, changes are still possible but costly. If a harried editor entitles an article "How to Improve Your Player Life" instead of "How to Improve Your Prayer Life," and no one notices it until the text has been at the printshop for two hours, the error will have to stand.

Ask that the completed pages be furnished *loose*. Printshops have specialized equipment that can automatically collate, fold, and bind your newsletter in a fraction of the time it would take human hands and a bank of staplers, if time is at a premium. If money is the problem, bring the completed pages back to the church to be transformed into a finished newsletter by willing volunteers, and save three to ten cents per copy.

Do not be overly insistent about deadlines. Rush jobs cost money and raise blood pressure. Give the printshop five working days on the average, a little less for loose pages only, a little more during December and the summer. Many newsletters, brochures, and magazines are published at the beginning of the month, so printshops are especially harried between the 25th and the 5th. Do not suggest weekend or evening work.

Do not aggravate or intimidate the printshop manager or attempt to impress him or her with your Christian commitment. If he is not a Christian, take every opportunity to be polite and hospitable, but avoid the urge to witness every time you drop off the newsletter copy. The newsletter text itself is witness enough.

After printing, collating, folding, and stapling the completed newsletter, the only step left is the mailing. Set aside those copies to be mailed, and staple them together once along the left front cover (to avoid the newsletter flying open at the post office).

Mailing labels can be created easily with most word processing programs, sorted by last name, first name, or zip code, and printed easily on laser printers (dot matrix printers are trickier, as usual). Run them off when you photocopy the text of the newsletter. When it comes time for mailing, simply affix the label (and a stamp, if the newsletter will not be mailed bulk rate). You may want to buy some sponges and rolls of stamps and add a "mailing" segment to the newsletter production party.

Getting Your Newsletter Involved

10

The newsletter has been written, edited, printed, and distributed. Your first impulse may be to dump the remaining copies onto that forgotten table in the sanctuary foyer next to tracts entitled "Should a Christian Vote for Jimmy Carter?" and "Disco: the Devil's Playground," and get on with the next issue. But the newsletter's job is just beginning. A few dozen or a few hundred extra copies can be put to work in the daily life of the church, hospital and shut-in visitation, personal evangelism, and community outreach.

In Sunday School and Church

Use newsletter articles to augment Sunday school lesson plans. An article on "Christian Depression" could form the basis of a discussion in high school, young adult, or adult classes. An article on "How to Really Enjoy the Old Testament" could augment any Bible study from Genesis to Malachi.

Prepare a special issue of the newsletter, written and edited primarily by children in a specific Sunday school class. Give each child a byline, and allow each child to take home a copy.

Send newsletters home with children whose parents do not attend church, even if the children don't have a byline.

Ask specific organizations to write, edit, or distribute issues of the newsletter.

Use newsletters with special themes to augment special programs. The Easter issue, for instance, could easily be distributed after the Easter cantata, and the Christmas issue during a Christmas program.

Use newsletters with special themes to honor specific segments of the church community. The Mother's Day issue could be distributed to honor mothers by modifying the mailing labels: *Mrs. Roberta Schwartz* instead of *Mr. and Mrs. Thomas Schwartz*. An issue devoted to children could be mailed to the children of the household instead of the parents.

Give newsletter subscriptions to members of the congregation who are away at college or seminary, who have moved to other cities, or who have left the church for any reason.

In Visitation

Instead of mailing newsletters to shut-ins, send them along with the visitation committee or the pastor.

Individuals in nursing and retirement homes may receive several copies to distribute to their friends.

Include several copies of the newsletter for the pastor to bring along on hospital visitation. Even those members who receive regular issues may be interested in getting a new copy of the newsletter while hospitalized.

Most hospital chapels keep copies of several different newsletters, brochures, and tracts for use of patients and staff. Ask the chaplain's permission before placing your church's newsletter among them.

Give a three-month newsletter subscription to anyone who visits the church, including those visiting from out of town.

Give a few back issues to anyone who joins the church.

Bring several copies of the newsletter on visits to new members, suggesting that they be used for personal evangelism.

In Personal Evangelism

Distribute copies of the newsletter in door-to-door canvassing efforts. Say, "We represent the _____ church down the block, and we're introducing ourselves to our neighbors."

Give a copy of the newsletter along with other materials to those who recently have become Christians.

Send copies of the newsletter along with letters to unchurched family and friends "just to let you know what I've been up to. . . ."

Leave a copy of the newsletter conspicuously placed on your desk at work (in the same location where your colleagues may leave their Danielle Steele novels).

"Accidentally" leave a copy of the newsletter in the employee or student lounge, in the doctor's waiting room, on the bus or subway, in your booth at the restaurant.

When you're approached by a street person, give him a quarter *and* a copy of the newsletter. Often the homeless appreciate having something easy to read.

Include "wrote for/edited/helped distribute church newsletter" on your resume under "Volunteer Activities."

In Community Outreach

Mail copies of the newsletter to other churches in your denomination, nearby churches of any denomination, and city-wide interreligious organizations. Do not forget college religious groups, such as the Navigators and Campus Crusade for Christ.

Bulletin boards open to all members of the community are available at supermarkets, drugstores, libraries, shopping malls, bus stations, parks, police stations, and elsewhere. Why not attach a copy of the newsletter? (Sometimes permission or a special stamp is required; check other material on the bulletin board.)

Put the management of local bars, adult bookstores, pornographic theaters, and other institutions on the newsletter's mailing list.

Put your mayor and city council members on the newsletter's mailing list.

Bring copies of the newsletter to rallies and political gatherings.

Restaurants often allow community magazines, rental advertisements, and brochures to be stacked on the floor or a table near the entrance (the secular equivalent of the church's traditional tract rack). There's no reason why your church newsletter couldn't be one of the free publications. Ask the manager's permission first; explain that you represent a nearby church and want to extend a neighborly invitation to his patrons. He may or may not examine a copy of the newsletter first, since some very odd and offensive groups have access to laser printers. In a popular establishment, twenty copies of *anything* will be gone in a single weekend.

Libraries, college student unions, campus religious centers, community centers, coffeehouses, women's centers, health clinics, recreation centers, and other public places often have similar piles of free literature. Make a monthly newsletter run of likely spots within a few miles of the church, dropping off between five and fifteen newsletters at each.

Appendix

Useful Books and Periodicals

Some of the best books are, unfortunately, out of print, but they should be available in larger public and seminary libraries—and they are worth the trouble of digging up.

1. Books about Newsletters

Anema, Durlynn C. *Designing Effective Brochures and Newsletters*. Dubuque, Iowa: Kendall Hunt (sub. of William C. Brown), 1991. Short but effective desk reference.

Arth, Marvin and Helen Ashmore. *The Newsletter Editor's Desk Book*. 3d ed. West Tisbury, Mass.: Parkway Printing Ltd., 1984.

Beach, Mark. *Editing Your Newsletter*. 3d ed. Portland, Oreg.: Coast to Coast Books, 1988. An excellent resource for starting from scratch, with many ideas on layout, graphics, and photos. Geared to the newsletters of businesses and industry.

Brigham, Nancy. *How to Do Leaflets, Newsletters and Newspapers*. Mamaroneck, N.Y.: Hastings, 1982.

Crockett, David W. *Promotion and Publicity for Churches*. Wilton, Conn.: Morehouse-Barlow, 1974. A general study, good for ideas about what your newsletter can do besides warm a table in the sanctuary foyer.

Darnay, Brigitte T., ed. *Newsletters in Print.* 4th ed. 1988-89. Detroit: Gale Research, Inc., 1988. A comprehensive listing of newsletters on a variety of topics, with contact information and subscription prices. The *Literary Market Place* of the newsletter business. Too expensive (and too superfluous) to warrant buying a copy, but go down to the library and at least have a look.

How to Start Publishing Newsletters. Vancouver, Wash.: Towers Club, 1990. Short, to the point.

Hudson, Howard. *Publishing Newsletters.* Rev. ed. New York: Macmillan, 1988. For professional newsletter editors, particularly those in business and industry.

Knight, George W. *How to Publish a Church Newsletter: An Illustrated Guide to First Class Editing, Design, and Production.* Rev. ed. Nashville: Broadman, 1989. George Knight is an expert on church newsletters. See his volumes of newsletter fillers and cartoons. Lots of practical hints on the nuts and bolts of the newsletter business.

McKinney, John. *How to Start Your Own Community Newspaper.* Port Jefferson, N.Y.: Meadow Press, 1977. McKinney's advice is often relevant to starting your own church newsletter, too.

Wales, LaRae H. *A Practical Guide to Newsletter Editing and Design.* 2d ed. Ames, Iowa: The Iowa State University Press, 1976. A little outdated. Skip the chapters on how to use a mimeograph machine. Sections on layout and typography are still useful.

Williams, Patricia A. *Creating and Producing the Perfect Newsletter.* Glenview, Ill.: Scott, Foresman & Company (sub. of Times, Inc.), 1989. As usual in the newsletter business, aimed toward editors in business and industry.

2. Books on Writing and Editing

Anderson, Margaret J. *The Christian Writer's Handbook.* Grand Rapids, Mich.: Zondervan, 1974. Rather dated, but still useful, and not as specialized as Ethel Herr's (see below).

The Associated Press Stylebook and Libel Manual: The Journalist's Bible. Rev. ed. New York: Addison-Wesley, 1987. Nice to have around for stylistic minutiae (e.g., should *hands off* be hyphenated? Is *Near East* or *Middle East* the approved term?). Buy *The Chicago Manual of Style* first, if you can afford it.

Austin, Charles. *Let the People Know*. Minneapolis: Augsburg, 1975. Covers all aspects of church publicity.

Bernstein, Theodore. *The Careful Writer: A Modern Guide to English Usage*. New York: Atheneum, 1977. Not revised recently, and therefore not particularly up-to-date, but a classic with nearly the exalted status of Strunk & White. Two thousand alphabetical entries. Feel free to break any of the rules Bernstein dictates, but first know what the rules *are*.

_____. *Miss Thistlebottom's Hobgoblins: The Careful Writer's Guide to the Taboos, Bugbears, and Outmoded Rules of English Usage*. New York: Simon and Schuster, 1984. Another classic, aimed at those writers and editors stifled by third-grade English "rules of correct grammar."

Brady, John. *The Craft of Interviewing*. Cincinnati: Writers Digest Books, 1977. Like most of the Writers Digest line, this book is 90 percent common sense, 10 percent ideas. A good refresher course anyway, or a primer on interviewing for the more timid members of the newsletter staff.

The Chicago Guide to Preparing Electronic Manuscripts. Chicago: The University of Chicago Press, 1987. Especially useful if your copy is going to be professionally typeset. To be used in conjunction with *The Chicago Manual of Style* (below).

The Chicago Manual of Style. Rev. ed. Chicago: The University of Chicago Press, 1982. No one who works with words can get along without the *Chicago Manual* for long. It is more comprehensive than the *Associated Press Stylebook* (Does the period go inside or outside the quotation marks?). Also, expensive and somewhat less user-friendly than the *Associated Press Stylebook*.

Crowell, Thomas Lee, Jr. *Index to Modern English*. New York: McGraw-Hill, 1964. A standard guide to English grammar, no better or worse than any other, but readily available.

Darcy, Laura and Louise Boston. *Webster's New World Dictionary of Computer Terms*. New York: Prentice-Hall 1988. Definitions of ANSI, JCL, NAND, NDRO, OROM, PSW, pulse-code modulation, and virtual address for serious hackers; DOS and modems for the rest of us.

Fedler, Fred. *Reporting for the Print Media: A Workbook*. 4th ed. New York: Harcourt Brace Jovanovich, 1988. A good resource for ideas and exercises for training fledgling newsletter writers.

Flesch, Rudolph. *The Art of Readable Writing*. New York: Harper and Row, 1949. Rev. ed. 1986. Don't let the pre-Eisenhower publication date fool you. Required reading for every writer and editor.

Fontaine, Andre and William A. Glavin, *The Art of Writing Non-Fiction*. 2d ed. Syracuse, N.Y.: Syracuse University Press, 1987. Not exactly newsletter writing, not exactly journalism: finding a topic, organization, research, interviewing, and writing for all types of nonfiction. Lively, informative.

Fredette, Jean M., ed. *Handbook of Magazine Article Writing*. Cincinnati: Writers Digest Books, 1988. Generating enthusiasm is the Writers Digest trademark, and these short essays will help stir your newsletter writers' apathy and give them some ideas for potential articles. Intended for freelance writers.

Gorrell, Robert M. and Charlton Laird. *Modern English Handbook*. 6th ed. Englewood Cliffs, N.J.: Prentice-Hall, 1976. Another of those grammar guides you had to buy for freshman composition class, and now need no more than twice a year. But, for those two times. . . .

Graves, Robert and Alan Hodge. *The Reader Over Your Shoulder*. 2d ed. New York: Vintage Books, 1979. Okay, so the examples are taken from such moderns as Winston Churchill. One of the few books on style that goes beyond old chestnuts like "avoid wordiness," written by two of the clearest and most invigorating writers of their generation.

Harriss, Julian, Kelly Leiter, and Stanley Johnson. *The Complete Reporter*. 5th ed. New York: Macmillan, 1985. An excellent, comprehensive guide, beginning with the five Ws and one H, and continuing through types of articles, researching, interviewing, copyediting, proofreading, and more. With exercises yet. Essential.

Herr, Ethel. *Introduction to Christian Writing*. 2d ed. Wheaton, Ill.: Tyndale House, 1988. Christian writers are all housewives sitting around the kitchen table writing poems about bear cubs who hibernate through Christmas! If you *are*, you'll like this book. If not, you can still pick up some pointers on types of articles to run and how to organize them.

Hodges, John C., and Mary E. Whitten. *Harbrace College Handbook*. 8th ed. New York: Harcourt Brace Jovanovich, 1977. Don't let the *college* in the title fool you; this is one of the more comprehensive grammar guides, in a handy format.

Kennedy, Bruce M. *Community Journalism: A Way of Life*. Ames, Iowa: The Iowa State University Press, 1974. *Extremely* dated, but anecdotal and fun. Especially valuable if you want to know exactly how printing and photography work.

Literary Market Place. New York: Bowker, 1940+. Annual. A thick, expensive directory of everything from publishing companies to freelance editors to paper suppliers. Consult the copy at your local library.

Plotnik, Arthur. *The Elements of Editing: A Modern Guide for Editors and Journalists*. New York: Macmillan, 1986. Supposed to take up where Strunk and White left off. Primarily for book and magazine editors.

Quirk, Randolph, and Sidney Greenbaum. *A Concise Grammar of Contemporary English*. New York: Harcourt Brace Jovanovich, 1974.

Skillen, Marjorie E. and Robert M. Gray. *Words into Type*. 3d ed. Englewood Cliffs, N.J.: Prentice-Hall 1986. A standard style manual for grammar, usage, style, and production methods. Some of the information on layout, typography, and printing is outdated, but much of it is still valid and valuable. To be consulted, not necessarily read.

Strunk, William, and E. B. White. *The Elements of Style*. 3d ed. New York: Macmillan, 1979. As the blurb says: "Buy it, study it, enjoy it." The best (and shortest) book on what makes writing good. Always in print, to be found in every bookstore, every library, and probably on the nightstand of every freelance writer, editor, and journalist in the business.

Sumrall, Velma and Lucille Germany. *Telling the Story of the Local Church: The Who, What, When, Where, and Why of Communication*. New York: Seabury, 1979.

Watkins, Floyd C., William B. Dillingham, and Edwin T. Martin. *Practical English Handbook*. 9th ed. Boston: Houghton Mifflin Co., 1992. A *Practical English Workbook* goes along with this book, in case you want to act as composition instructor to the newsletter staff.

Williams, Barbara. *Public Relations Handbook for Your Church*. Valley Forge, Penn.: Judson Press, 1985.

Zinsser, William. *On Writing Well: An Informal Guide to Writing Non-Fiction*. 3d ed. New York: HarperCollins, 1985. A little pretentious, but well on its way to classic status. William Zinsser has recently edited a number of fascinating analyses of different types of writing, including religious writing.

3. Books on Computers and Word Processing Systems

Benton, Randi and Mary Schenck Balcer. *The Official Print Shop Handbook: Ideas, Tips and Designs for Home, School and Professional Use*. New York: Bantam Books, 1987. Many useful templates and graphics ideas for the Print Shop software. Applications for both Macintosh and IBM PC users.

Compute's Quick and Easy Guide to Desktop Publishing. Greensboro, N.C.: Compute Publications, 1987. A brief, handy guide, a little dated by now, but then, what in the computer world isn't?

Davis, Frederic E., John A. Burry, and Martin L. W. Hall. *Newsletter Publishing with PageMaker*. Homewood, Ill.: Dow Jones-Irwin, 1988. Editions for both the Macintosh and the IBM PC.

Felici, James and Ted Nace. *Desktop Publishing Skills*. Reading, Mass.: Addison-Wesley, 1987.

Harvey, Greg and Kay Yarborough Nelson, *WordPerfect 5 Desktop Companion*. San Francisco: Sybex, 1988. Thick, expensive, but worth it. Goes beyond the basic dictionary format that many word processing manuals stubbornly cling to.

Kleper, Michael L. *The Illustrated Handbook of Desktop Publishing and Typesetting*. 2d ed. Blue Ridge Summit, Pa.: TAB Professional and Reference Books, 1990. Large (I mean huge), detailed, and technical. Maybe a bit too technical, but worth a glance at the library.

Labow, Martha and Polly Pattison, *Style Sheets for Newsletters*. Thousand Oaks, Calif.: New Riders Publishing Co, 1988. For Xerox Ventura customers.

Parker, Roger C. *Desktop Publishing with WordPerfect*. Chapel Hill, N.C.: Ventura Press, 1988. A little elementary. If you still have the reference manual that came with the WordPerfect diskettes, you probably don't need this book.

Ranley, Donald. *Publications Editing*. Ames, Iowa: The Iowa State University Press, 1991.

Stockford, James, Editor. *Desktop Publishing Bible*. Indianapolis: Howard W. Sams, 1987. Comprehensive, but unfortunately out of date. A revision should be appearing any moment now.

Ulick, Terry. *Personal Publishing with PC Pagemaker.* Indianapolis: Howard W. Sams, 1987. A comprehensive, up-to-date guide for Macintosh users.

Will-Harris, Daniel. *WordPerfect 5: Desktop Publishing in Style.* Berkeley, Calif.: Peachpit Press, 1988. Useful, sparkling, and entertaining (quite a novelty in desktop publishing manuals).

4. Research Sources

The Associated Church Press, P. O. Box 306, 321 James Street, Geneva, IL 60134. A non-evangelical religious news service. Offers workshops, research in Christian journalism, and awards.

The Associated Press, 50 Rockefeller Plaza, New York NY 10020. (212) 621-1500. The largest news service in the world, serving 1,400 newspapers and 3,900 radio and TV stations. No religious news desk, unfortunately, but lots of religious stories go through the wires.

Barton, Mary N., and Marion V. Bell. *Reference Books: A Brief Guide.* 8th ed. Baltimore: Enoch Pratt Free Library, 1978. Hard to find.

Barzun, Jacques and Henry Graff. *The Modern Researcher.* 4th ed. New York: Harcourt Brace Jovanovich, 1985. Slanted toward historians and social scientists, but valuable for everyone who has to use a library.

CompuServe, Inc., 5000 Arlington Centre Boulevard, Columbus, OH 43220. (800) 848-8990. The best of many on-line database research services.

Downs, Robert B., and Clara D. Keller. *How to Do Library Research.* 2d ed. Urbana, Ill.: University of Illinois Press, 1975. A standard textbook.

The Evangelical Press Association, c/o Gary Warner, Box 4550, Overland Park, KS 66205. Publishes the *Evangelical Press News Service* (weekly) and *Liaison* (bimonthly). Also offers a placement service and awards for evangelical Christian journalism.

Facts on File: World News Digest with Index. New York: Facts on File, 1940+. Weekly, with annual bound volumes available. Mainly for political and economic information.

McCormick, Mona. *New York Times Guide to Reference Materials.* 2d ed. New York: New American Library, 1986. The standard introduction to reference sources.

The National Christian Reporter, Box 222198, Dallas, TX 75222. (214) 630-6495. A weekly newspaper running many good short articles and fillers.

National Newspaper Index. Los Altos, Calif.: Information Access Corporation, 1979+. Monthly microfilm index of the *New York Times*, the *Wall Street Journal*, the *Christian Science Monitor*, the *Los Angeles Times*, and the *Washington Post*.

Readers' Guide to Periodical Literature. New York: Wilson, 1900+. Semimonthly, monthly, and annual indexes. Not for specialists, but helpful to find the article you remember reading in *Good Housekeeping* two years ago—fast.

Religion Index One: Periodicals. Chicago: American Theological Library Association, 1953+. Semiannual. Not evangelical in orientation, but comprehensive.

Religion Index Two: Multi-Author Works. Chicago: American Theological Library Association, 1978+. Annual.

Religious News Service, 43 West 57th Street, New York, NY 10019. Affiliated with the National Council of Christians and Jews (NCCJ), although most of the news stories deal with general religious issues rather than interfaith cooperation. Offers daily news reports, a photo service.

Sheehy, Eugene P. *Guide to Reference Books*. 10th ed. Chicago: American Library Association, 1986. An excellent companion for exploring new fields of knowledge.

Who's Who in America. Chicago: Marquis, 1899+. Biennial. Marquis also publishes regional and occupationally oriented Who's Whos, as well as a *Who Was Who* for persons no longer living.

5. Magazines and Newsletters

Christian Authors Newsletter, Christian Writers Institute, 388 E. Gundersen Drive, Wheaton, IL 60188. (312) 653-4200. Concentrates on freelance writing, but offers useful encouragement and advice for any writer.

Christian Writers' Newsletter, P.O. Box 8220, Knoxville, TN 37996-4800. Bimonthly.

Editor and Publisher, 11 West 19th Street, New York, NY 10011. The newspaper editor's trade weekly. Not always relevant to church newsletters; read the copy in the public library.

The Editorial Eye, Editorial Experts, Inc., 66 Canal Center Plaza, #200, Alexandria, VA 22314-1578. A reasonably priced eight-page newsletter containing useful and interesting short articles on desktop publishing, grammar, management, and writing style. Church newsletter editors will profit from a subscription.

Editors' Forum, P. O. Box 411806, Kansas City, MO 64141. (913) 236-9235.

Interlit, David C. Cook Foundation, Cook Square, Elgin, IL 60120. (708) 741-2400. A quarterly for evangelical journalists, editors, and publishers.

N-A Newsletter for Newsletters, Poll Communications Group, 200 Aldrich Avenue South, Minneapolis, MN 55404. (612) 872-9130.

Newsletter Design, 44 W. Market Street, P. O. Box 311, Rhinebeck, NY 12572. (914) 876-2081. A rather hefty subscription price will be prohibitive for anyone but professionals. Local business schools and colleges may have subscriptions. Try the same address and telephone number (and same subscription price caveat) for *The Newsletter on Newsletters*.

Personal Publishing, 25W559 Geneva Road, Wheaton, IL 60188-2292. (800) 627-7201. A desktop publishing monthly.

Publish, the Magazine for Graphic Communicators, 501 Second Street, San Francisco, CA 94107. (415) 546-7722. A little technical. Read a few copies at the library or newsstand to decide whether you really need it or not.

WordPerfect Magazine, WordPerfect Corporation, 270 West Center Street, Orem, UT 84057. (801) 226-5556. A humorous, well-produced glossy, geared to word processing professionals. Sometimes has interesting tips.

The Writer, 120 Boylston Street, Boston, MA 02116. A magazine for new writers, sometimes coddling and obvious, but nice to give the real new writers on your staff.

6. Newsletter Resources Published by Baker Book House

De Jong, Benjamin R. *Uncle Ben's Instant Clip-Quotes.*

Eddings, Eddie. *Laugh and Learn Cartoon Features for Church Publications.*

Flynn, Leslie B. and Bernice. *Humorous Incidents and Quips for Church Publications.*

Hall, Doug. *Cartoon Reflections: Church Humor for Newsletters and Bulletins.*

Jackson, Phil. *Ready-to-Use Cartoons for Church Publications 1-2.*

Knight, George W. *Church Bulletin Bits 1-4.*

_____. *Clip-Art Features for Church Newsletters 1-6.*

_____. *Clip Art Mini-Fillers for Church Publications.*

_____. *Clip-Art Sentence Sermons for Church Publications 1-2.*

_____. *Instant Cartoons for Church Newsletters 1- 6.*

McKeever, Joe, and George W. Knight, *Clip-Art Announcement Panels.*

McKenzie, C.E. *Mack's Church Publication Quotebook 1-2.*

_____. *Quips and Quotes for Church Bulletins.*

Mitchell, Roy. *God Is . . .: Cartoons Showing the Character of God (And How We Respond to Him).*

Paris, Howard. *Clip-Art Panel Cartoons for Churches 2-3.*

Wheeler, Ron. *Cartoon Clip-Art for Youth Leaders 1-2.*

7. Other Resources

Aldus Corporation, 411 First Avenue South, Suite 200, Seattle, WA 98104. (206) 662-5500. Source for PageMaker, FreeHand, and other software packages for Macintosh computers.

Apple Computers, 20525 Mariani Avenue, Cupertino, CA 95014. (408) 996-1010. Source for the Apple Macintosh, as well as a number of excellent software packages (MacWrite, MacDraw, etc.).

Canon USA, One Canon Plaza, Lake Success, NY 11042. The best (and until recently the only) place to get laser printers.

Hercules Computer Technology, 2550 Ninth Street, Berkeley, CA 94710. Excellent color graphics boards for creating your own on-screen art. You'll need a color monitor and extra funds in the newsletter budget for printing.

Hewlett Packard, 974 E. Arques Avenue, Sunnyvale, CA 94088. (800) 367-4772. Source for dot matrix and laser printers, as well as a software package, HP-Word. Regional offices throughout the United States and Canada.

IBM Corporation, P. O. Box 1328, Boca Raton, FL 33432. Manufacturers of IBM personal computers.

New Vision Technologies, Inc., 38 Auriga Drive #13, Nepean, Ontario, Canada K2E 8A5. (613) 727-8184. New Vision offers 650 color and 450 monochrome pieces of clip-art compatible with most systems: enough to keep your newsletter fresh and innovative for years. Many are not appropriate for churches. Ask for their catalog.

Reasonable Solutions, 2101 West Main Street, Medford, OR 97501. (800) 876-3475. Offers computer-generated clip-art, with emphasis on church-related images (#2615). Also many useful utility programs, not to mention a reasonably-priced on-line King James Bible (#3170).

WordPerfect Corporation, 270 West Center Street, Orem, UT 84057. (801) 226-5556. Publishes WordPerfect 5.0 and 5.1, DrawPerfect, and other software packages, as well as the useful and entertaining *WordPerfect Magazine.*